Forgotten Books

Barrack-Room Ballads and Ditties

By

Rudyard Kipling

Published by Forgotten Books 2012

PIBN 1000610570

Rudyard Kipling

Barrack-Room
Ballads and
Ditties

PHILADELPHIA
HENRY ALTEMUS

CONTENTS.

CONTENTS.

PAGE

CONTENTS.

PAGE

CONTENTS. vii

I HAVE eaten your bread and salt,
* I have drunk your water and wine,*
The deaths ye died I have watched beside,
* And the lives that ye led were mine.*

Was there aught that I did not share
* In vigil or toil or ease,—*
One joy or woe that I did not know,
* Dear hearts across the seas ?*

I have written the tale of our life
* For a sheltered people's mirth,*
In jesting guise—but ye are wise,
* And ye know what the jest is worth.*

General Summary.

WE are very slightly changed
From the semi-apes who ranged
   India's prehistoric clay;
Whoso drew the longest bow,
Ran his brother down, you know,
   As we run men down to-day.

"Dowb," the first of all his race,
Met the Mammoth face to face
   On the lake or in the cave,
Stole the steadiest canoe,
Ate the quarry others slew,
   Died—and took the finest grave.

When they scratched the reindeer-bone,
Some one made the sketch his own,
   Filched it from the artist—then,
Even in those early days,
Won a simple Viceroy's praise
   Through the toil of other men.

Ere they hewed the Sphinx's visage
Favoritism governed kissage,
Even as it does in this age.

Who shall doubt the secret hid
Under Cheops' pyramid
Was that the contractor did
    Cheops out of several millions?
Or that Joseph's sudden rise
To Comptroller of Supplies
Was a fraud of monstrous size
    On King Pharaoh's swart Civilians?

Thus, the artless songs I sing
Do not deal with anything
    New or never said before.
As it was in the beginning,
Is to-day official sinning,
    And shall be for evermore.

Danny Deever.

"WHAT are the bugles blowin' for?" said
　Files-on-Parade.
"To turn you out, to turn you out," the
　Color-Sergeant said.
"What makes you look so white, so white?"
　said Files-on-Parade.
"I'm dreadin' what I've got to watch," the
　Color-Sergeant said.
　　For they're hangin' Danny Deever,
　　　you can 'ear the Dead March play,
　　The regiment's in 'ollow square—
　　　they're hangin' him to-day;
　　They've taken of his buttons off an'
　　　cut his stripes away,
　　An' they're hangin' Danny Deever in
　　　the mornin'.

"What makes the rear-rank breathe so 'ard?"
　said Files-on-Parade.
"It's bitter cold, it's bitter cold," the Color-
　Sergeant said.
"What makes that front-rank man fall
　down?" said Files-on-Parade.

"A touch of sun, a touch of sun," the Color-
Sergeant said.
> They are hangin' Danny Deever, they
> are marchin' of 'im round,
> They 'ave 'alted Danny Deever by 'is
> coffin on the ground;
> An' 'e'll swing in 'arf a minute for a
> sneakin', shootin' hound—
> O they're hangin' Danny Deever in
> the mornin'!

"'Is cot was right-'and cot to mine," said
Files-on-Parade.
"'E's sleepin' out an' far to-night," the Color-
Sergeant said.
"I've drunk 'is beer a score o' times," said
Files-on-Parade.
"'E's drinkin' bitter beer alone," the Color-
Sergeant said.
> They are hangin' Danny Deever, you
> must mark 'im to 'is place,
> For 'e shot a comrade sleepin'—you
> must look 'im in the face;
> Nine 'undred of 'is county an' the
> regiment's disgrace,
> While they're hangin' Danny Deever
> in the mornin'.

'What's that so black agin the sun?" said
  Files-on-Parade.
'It's Danny fightin' 'ard for life," the Color-
  Sergeant said.
"What's that that whimpers over'ead?" said
  Files-on-Parade.
"It's Danny's soul that's passin' now," the
  Color-Sergeant said.

    For they're done with Danny Deever,
      you can 'ear the quickstep play,
    The regiment's in column, an' they're
      marchin' us away;
    Ho! the young recruits are shakin',
      an' they'll want their beer to-day,
    After hangin' Danny Deever in the
      mornin'.

Army Headquarters.

OLD is the song that I sing—
　　Old as my unpaid bills—
　　Old as the chicken that *kitmutgars* bring
　　Men at dak-bungalows—old as the Hills.

AHASUERUS JENKINS of the " Operatic
Own "
Was dowered with a tenor voice of *super-*
Santley tone.
His views on equitation were, perhaps, a
trifle queer;
He had no seat worth mentioning, but oh !
he had an ear.

He clubbed his wretched company a dozen
times a day,
He used to quit his charger in a parabolic
way,
His method of saluting was the joy of all
beholders,
But Ahasuerus Jenkins had a head upon his
shoulders.
He took two months to Simla when the year
was at the spring,
(16)

And underneath the deodars eternally did
sing.
He warbled like a *bulbul*, but particularly at
Cornelia Agrippina who was musical and
fat.

She controlled a humble husband, who, in
turn, controlled a Dept.,
Where Cornelia Agrippina's human singing-
birds were kept
From April to October on a plump retaining
fee,
Supplied, of course, *per mensem*, by the In-
dian Treasury.

Cornelia used to sing with him, and Jenkins
used to play ·
He praised unblushingly her notes, for he
was false as they :
So when the winds of April turned the bud-
ding roses brown,
Cornelia told her husband:—"Tom, you
mustn't send him down."

They haled him from his regiment which
didn't much regret him ;
They found for him an office-stool, and on
that stool they set him,

To play with maps and catalogues three idle
   hours a day,
And draw his plump retaining fee—which
   means his double pay.

Now, ever after dinner, when the coffee-cups
   are brought,
Ahasuerus waileth o'er the grand pianoforte;
And, thanks to fair Cornelia, his fame hath
   waxen great,
And Ahasuerus Jenkins is a power in the
   ·State.

A Legend of the Foreign Office.

THIS is the reason why Rustum Beg,
    Rajah of Kolazai,
Drinketh the " simpkin " and brandy peg,
    Maketh the money to fly,
Vexeth a Government, tender and kind,
Also—but this is a detail—blind.

RUSTUM BEG of Kolazai—slightly back-
    ward native State—
Lusted for a C. S. I.,—so began to sanitate.
Built a Jail and Hospital—nearly built a
    City drain—
Till his faithful subjects all thought their
    ruler was insane.

Strange departures made he then—yea, De-
    partments stranger still,
Half a dozen Englishmen helped the Rajah
    with a will,
Talked of noble aims and high, hinted of a
    future fine
For the state of Kolazai, on a strictly West-
    ern line.

Rajah Rustum held his peace; lowered
 octroi dues a half;
Organized a State Police; purified the
 Civil Staff;
Settled cess and tax afresh in a very liberal
 way;
Cut temptations of the .flesh—also cut the
 Bukhshi's pay;

Roused his Secretariat to a fine Mahratta
 fury,
By a Hookum hinting at supervision of
 dasturi;
Turned the State of Kolazai very nearly up-
 side down;
When the end of May was nigh, waited his
 achievement crown.
Then the Birthday Honors came. Sad to
 state and sad to see,
Stood against the Rajah's name nothing
 more than *C. I. E. !*

. . . . .

Things were lively for a week in the State
 of Kolazai.
Even now the people speak of that time re-
 gretfully.

How he disendowed the Jail—stopped at
  once the City drain;
Turned to beauty fair and frail—got his
  senses back again;
Doubled taxes, cesses, all; cleared away each
  new-built *thana;*
Turned the two-lakh Hospital into a superb
  Zenana;

Heaped upon the Bukhshi Sahib wealth and
  honors manifold;
Clad himself in Eastern garb—squeezed his
  people as of old.
Happy, happy Kolazai! Never more will
  Rustum Beg
Play to catch the Viceroy's eye. He prefers
  the "simpkin" peg.

The Story of Uriah.

"Now there were two men in one city; the one rich and the other poor."

JACK BARRETT went to Quetta
  Because they told him to.
He left his wife at Simla
  On three-fourths his monthly screw:
Jack Barrett died at Quetta
  Ere the next month's pay he drew.

Jack Barrett went to Quetta.
  He didn't understand
The reason of his transfer
  From the pleasant mountain-land:
The season was September,
  And it killed him out of hand.

Jack Barrett went to Quetta,
  And there gave up the ghost,
Attempting two men's duty
  In that very healthy post;
And Mrs. Barrett mourned for him
  Five lively months at most.

(22)

Jack Barrett's bones at Quetta
   Enjoy profound repose;
But I shouldn't be astonished
   If *now* his spirit knows
The reason of his transfer
   From the Himalayan snows.

And, when the Last Great Bugle Call
   Adown the Hurnai throbs,
When the last grim joke is entered
   In the big black Book of Jobs,
And Quetta graveyards give again
   Their victims to the air,
I shouldn't like to be the man
   Who sent Jack Barrett there.

The Post that Fitted.

THOUGH tangled and twisted the course of true love,
    This ditty explains
No tangle's so tangled it cannot improve
    If the Lover has brains.

ERE the steamer bore him Eastward, Sleary
    was engaged to marry
An attractive girl at Tunbridge, whom he
    called "my little Carrie."
Sleary's pay was very modest; Sleary was
    the other way.
Who can cook a two-plate dinner on eight
    paltry dibs a day?

Long he pondered o'er the question in his
    scantly-furnished quarters—
Then proposed to Minnie Boffkin, eldest of
    Judge Boffkin's daughters.
Certainly an impecunious Subaltern was not
    a catch,
But the Boffkins knew that Minnie mightn't
    make another match.

(24)

So they recognized the business, and, to feed
　and clothe the bride,
Got him made a Something Something some-
　where on the Bombay side.
Anyhow, the billet carried pay enough for
　him to marry—
As the artless Sleary put it:—"Just the
　thing for me and Carrie."

Did he, therefore, jilt Miss Boffkin—im-
　pulse of a baser mind?
No! He started epileptic fits of an appall-
　ing kind.
(Of his *modus operandi* only this much I
　could gather:—
"Pears' shaving sticks will give you little
　taste and lots of lather.")

Frequently in public places his affliction
　used to smite
Sleary with distressing vigor—always in the
　Boffkins' sight.
Ere a week was over Minnie weepingly re-
　turned his ring,
Told him his "unhappy weakness" stopped
　all thought of marrying.

Sleary bore the information with a chastened
    holy joy,—
Epileptic fits don't matter in Political em-
    ploy,—
Wired three short words to Carrie—took his
    ticket, packed his kit—
Bade farewell to Minnie Boffkin in one last,
    long, lingering fit.

Four weeks later, Carrie Sleary read—and
    laughed until she wept—
Mrs. Boffkin's warning letter on the
    "wretched epilept."
Year by year, in pious patience, vengeful
    Mrs. Boffkin sits
Waiting for the Sleary babies to develop
    Sleary's fits.

Delilah.

WE have another Viceroy now, those days are dead and done,
Of Delilah Aberyswith and depraved Ulysses Gunne.

DELILAH ABERYSWITH was a lady—
  not too young—
With a perfect taste in dresses, and a badly-
  bitted tongue,
With a thirst for information, and a greater
  thirst for praise,
And a little house in Simla, in the Prehis-
  toric Days.

By reason of her marriage to a gentleman
  in power,
Delilah was acquainted with the gossip of
  the hour;
And many little secrets, of a half-official
  kind,
Were whispered to Delilah, and she bore
  them all in mind.

She patronized extensively a man, Ulysses
  Gunne,
Whose mode of earning money was a low
  and shameful one.

He wrote for divers papers, which, as every-
 body knows,
Is worse than serving in a shop or scaring
 off the crows.

He praised her " queenly beauty " first; and,
 later on, he hinted
At the " vastness of her intellect " with com-
 pliment unstinted.
He went with her a-riding, and his love for
 her was such
That he lent her all his horses, and—she
 galled them very much.

One day, THEY brewed a secret of a fine finan-
 cial sort;
It related to Appointments, to a Man and a
 Report.
'Twas almost worth the keeping (only seven
 people knew it),
And Gunne rose up to seek the truth and
 patiently pursue it.

It was a Viceroy's Secret, but—perhaps the
 wine was red—
Perhaps an aged Councillor had lost his aged
 head—

Perhaps Delilah's eyes were bright—Delilah's
   whispers sweet—
The Aged Member told her what 'twere trea-
   son to repeat.

Ulysses went a-riding, and they talked of
   love and flowers;
Ulysses went a-calling, and he called for
   several hours;
Ulysses went a-waltzing, and Delilah helped
   him dance—
Ulysses let the waltzes go, and waited for his
   chance.

The summer sun was setting, and the sum-
   mer air was still,
The couple went a-walking in the shade of
   Summer Hill,
The wasteful sunset faded out in turkis-green
   and gold,
Ulysses pleaded softly, and . . . that bad
   Delilah told !

Next morn, a startled Empire learnt the all-
   important news;
Next week, the Aged Councillor was shak
   ing in his shoes;

Next month, I met Delilah, and she did not
show the least
Hesitation in affirming that Ulysses was a
" beast."

   .   .   .   .   .

We have another Viceroy now, those days
are dead and done,
Of Delilah Aberyswith and most mean
Ulysses Gunne!

Pink Dominoes.

" THEY are fools who kiss and tell "
Wisely has the poet sung.
Man may hold all sorts of posts
If he'll only hold his tongue.

JENNY and Me were engaged, you see,
　On the eve of the Fancy Ball;
So a kiss or two was nothing to you
　Or any one else at all.

Jenny would go in a domino—
　Pretty and pink but warm;
While I attended, clad in a splendid
　Austrian uniform.

Now we had arranged, through notes ex·
　changed
　Early that afternoon,
At Number Four to waltz no more,
　But to sit in the dusk and spoon.

(I wish you to see that Jenny and Me
　Had barely exchanged our troth;
So a kiss or two was strictly due
　By, from, and between us both.)

(31)

When Three was over, an eager lover,
   I fled to the gloom outside;
And a Domino came out also
   Whom I took for my future bride.

That is to say, in a casual way,
   I slipped my arm around her;
With a kiss or two (which is nothing to you),
   And ready to kiss I found her.

She turned her head, and the name she said
   Was certainly not my own;
But ere I could speak, with a smothered
     shriek
She fled and left me alone.

Then Jenny came, and I saw with shame
   She'd doffed her domino;
And I had embraced an alien waist—
   But I did not tell her so.

Next morn I knew that there were two
   Dominoes pink, and one
Had cloaked the spouse of Sir Julian Vouse,
   Our big political gun.

Sir J. was old, and her hair was gold,
    And her eye was a blue cerulean;
And the name she said when she turned her
    head
Was not in the least like " Julian."

Now wasn't it nice, when want of *pice*
    Forbade us twain to marry,
That old Sir J., in the kindest way,
    Made me his Secre*tarry ?*

The Man who could Write.

SHUN—shun the Bowl! That fatal, facile drink
  Has ruined many geese who dipped their quills in't;
Bribe, murder, marry, but steer clear of Ink
  Save when you write receipts for paid-up bills in't.
There may be silver in the "blue-black"—all
I know of is the iron and the gall.

BOANERGES BLITZEN, servant of the
  Queen,
Is a dismal failure—is a Might-have-been.
In a luckless moment he discovered men
Rise to high position through a ready pen.

Boanerges Blitzen argued, therefore: " I
With the selfsame weapon can attain as
  high."
Only he did not possess, when he made the
  trial,
Wicked wit of C-lv-n, irony of L   l.

(Men who spar with Government need, to
  back their blows,
Something more than ordinary journalistic
  prose.)
  (34)

Never young Civilian's prospects were so
    bright,
Till an Indian paper found that he could
    write ;
Never young Civilian's prospects were so
    dark, '
When the wretched Blitzen wrote to make
    his mark.

Certainly re scored it. bold and black and
    firm,
In that Indian paper—made his seniors
    squirm,
Quoted office scandals, wrote the tactless
    truth—
Was there ever known a more misguided
    youth ?

When the rag he wrote for praised his plucky
    game,
Boanerges Blitzen felt that this was Fame;
When the men he wrote of shook their heads
    and swore,
Boanerges Blitzen only wrote the more.

Posed as Young Ithuriel, resolute and grim,
Till he found promotion didn't come to
    him ;

Till he found that reprimands weekly were
 his lot,
And his many Districts curiously hot.

Till he found his furlough strangely hard to
 win,
Boanerges Blitzen didn't care a pin:
Then it seemed to dawn on him something
 wasn't right—
Boanerges Blitzen put it down to "spite."

Languished in a District desolate and dry;
Watched the Local Government yearly pass
 him by;
Wondered where the hitch was; called it
 most unfair.

  . . . . .

That was seven years ago—and he still is
 there.

Municipal.

"WHY is my District death-rate low?"
   Said Binks of Hezabad.
" Wells, drains, and sewage-outfalls are
   My own peculiar fad.
I learnt a lesson once. It ran
   Thus," quoth that most veracious man :—

IT was an August evening, and, in snowy
   garments clad,
I paid a round of visits in the lines of Heza-
   bad;
When, presently, my Waler saw, and did
   not like at all,
A Commissariat Elephant careering down
   the Mall.

I couldn't see the driver, and across my
   mind it rushed
That the Commissariat elephant had sud-
   denly gone *musth*.
I didn't care to meet him, and I couldn't
   well get down,
So I let the Waler have it and we headed for
   the town.

The buggy was a new one, and, praise
Dykes, it stood the strain,
Till the Waler jumped a bullock just above
the City Drain,
And the next that I remember was a hurri-
cane of squeals,
And the creature making toothpicks of my
five-foot patent wheels.

He seemed to want the owner, so I fled, dis-
traught with fear,
To the Main Drain sewage-outfall while he
snorted in my ear—
Reached the four-foot drain-head safely,
and, in darkness and despair,
Felt the brute's proboscis fingering my ter-
ror-stiffened hair.

Heard it trumpet on my shoulder—tried to
crawl a little higher—
Found the Main Drain sewage-outfall
blocked, some eight feet up, with mire;
And, for twenty reeking minutes, Sir, my
very marrow froze,
While the trunk was feeling blindly for a
purchase on my toes!

It missed me by a fraction, but my hair was
    turning gray
Before they called the drivers up and
    dragged the brute away.
Then I sought the City Elders, and my
    words were very plain.
They flushed that four-foot drain-head, and
    —it never choked again.

You may hold with surface-drainage, and
    the sun for garbage-cure,
Till you've been a periwinkle shrinking
    coyly up a sewer.
I believe in well-flushed culverts . . . .
      This is why the death-rate's small ;
And, if you don't believe me, get *shikarred*
    yourself. That's all.

A Code of Morals.

Lest you should think this story true,
I merely mention I
Evolved it lately. 'Tis a most
Unmitigated misstatement.

NOW Jones had left his new-wed bride to
keep his house in order,
And hied away to the Hurrum Hills above
the Afghan border,
To sit on a rock with a heliograph ; but ere
he left he taught
His wife the working of the Code that sets
the miles at naught.

And Love had made him very sage, as Na-
ture made her fair ;
So Cupid and Apollo linked, *per* heliograph,
the pair.
At dawn, across the Hurrum Hills, he
flashed her counsel wise—
At e'en, the dying sunset bore her husband's
homilies.

(40)

He warned her 'gainst seductive youths in
    scarlet clad and gold,
As much as 'gainst the blandishments pa-
    ternal of the old ;
But kept his gravest warnings for (hereby
    the ditty hangs)
That   snowy-haired Lothario, Lieutenant-
    General Bangs.

'Twas General Bangs, with Aide and Staff,
    that tittupped on the way,
When they beheld a heliograph tempestu-
    ously at play ;
They thought of Border risings, and of sta-
    tions sacked and burnt—
So stopped to take the message down—and
    this is what they learnt :—

" Dash dot dot, dot, dot dash, dot dash dot"
    twice.   The General swore.
"Was   ever General Officer addressed as
    ' dear ' before?
'My Love,' i' faith ! 'My Duck,' Gadsooks!
    'My darling popsy-wop !'
Spirit of great Lord Wolseley, *who* is on that
    mountain top ?"

The artless Aide-de-camp was mute; the
　　gilded Staff were still,
As, dumb with pent-up mirth, they booked
　　that message from the hill;
For, clear as summer's lightning flare, the
　　husband's warning ran:
" Don't dance or ride with General Bangs—
　　a most immoral man."

(At dawn, across the Hurrum Hills, he
　　flashed her counsel wise—
But, howsoever Love be blind, the world at
　　·large hath eyes.)
With damnatory dot and dash he helio-
　　graphed his wife
Some interesting details of the General's
　　private life.

The artless Aide-de-camp was mute; the
　　shining Staff were still,
And red and ever redder grew the General's
　　shaven gill.
And this is what he said at last (his feelings
　　matter not):—
" I think we've tapped a private line. Hi!
　　Threes about there! Trot!"

All honor unto Bangs, for ne'er did Jones
    thereafter know
By word or act official who read of that
    helio. ;
But the tale is on the Frontier, and from
    Michni to Mool*tan*
They know the worthy General as "that
    most immoral man."

"Tommy."

I WENT into a public-'ouse to get a pint o'
    beer,   .
The publican 'e up an' sez, "We serve no
    redcoats here."
The girls be'ind the bar they laughed an'
    giggled fit to die,
I outs into the street again, an' to myself
    sez I:

    O it's Tommy this, an' Tommy that, an'
        "Tommy go away;"
    But it's "Thank you, Mister Atkins,"
        when the band begins to play,
    The band begins to play, my boys, the
        band begins to play,
    O it's "Thank you, Mister Atkins,"
        when the band begins to play.

I went into a theatre as sober as could be,
They give a drunk civilian room, but 'adn't
    none for me;
They sent me to the gallery or round the
    music-'alls,
But when it comes to fightin', Lord! they'll
    shove me in the stalls.

For it's Tommy this, an' Tommy that,
    an' "Tommy wait outside;"
But it's "Special train for Atkins," when
    the trooper's on the tide,
The troopship's on the tide, my boys,
    etc.

O makin' mock o' uniforms that guard you
    while you sleep
Is cheaper than them uniforms, an' they're
    starvation cheap,
An' hustlin' drunken sodgers when they're
    goin' large a bit
Is five times better business than paradin'
    in full kit.
    Then it's Tommy this, an' Tommy that,
        an' "Tommy, 'ow's yer soul?"
    But it's "Thin red line of 'eroes" when
        the drums begin to roll,
    The drums begin to roll, my boys, etc.

We aren't no thin red 'eroes, nor we aren't
    no blackguards too,
But single men in barricks, most remarka-
    ble like you; .

An' if sometimes our conduck isn't all your
    fancy paints,
Why, single men in barricks don't grow into
    plaster saints.
      While it's Tommy this, an' Tommy that,
        an' " Tommy fall be'ind ;"
      But it's " Please to walk in front, sir,"
        when there's trouble in the wind,
      There's trouble in the wind, my boys,
        etc.

You talk o' better food for us, an' schools,
    an' fires, an' all :
We'll wait for extry rations if you treat us
    rational.
Don't mess about the cook-room slops, but
    prove it to our face
The Widow's uniform is not the soldier-
    man's disgrace.
      For it's Tommy this, an' Tommy that,
        an' " Chuck him out, the brute!"
      But it's " Saviour of 'is country " when
        the guns begin to shoot ;
      An' it's Tommy this, an' Tommy that,
        an' anything you please ;
      An' Tommy ain't a bloomin' fool—you
        bet that Tommy sees !

"Fuzzy-Wuzzy."

(Soudan Expeditionary Force.)

WE'VE fought with many men acrost the
    seas,
    An' some of 'em was brave an' some was
      not :
The Paythan an' the Zulu an' Burmese ;
    But the Fuzzy was the finest o' the lot.
We never got a ha'porth's change of 'im :
    'E squatted in the scrub an' 'ocked our
      'orses,
'E cut our sentries up at Sua*kim*,
    An' 'e played the cat an' banjo with our
      forces.
        So 'ere's *to* you, Fuzzy-Wuzzy, at your
          'ome in the Sowdan ;
        You're a poor benighted 'eathen but a
          first-class fightin' man ;
        We gives you your certifikit, and if
          you want it signed
        We'll come an' 'ave a romp with you
          whenever you're inclined.

We took our chanst among the Kyber hills,
  The Boers knocked us silly at a mile,
The Burman guv us Irriwaddy chills,
  An' a Zulu *impi* dished us up in style;
But all we ever got from such as they
  Was pop to what the Fuzzy made us swal-
    ler;
We 'eld our bloomin' own, the papers say,
  But man for man the Fuzzy knocked us
    'oller.
        Then 'ere's *to* you, Fuzzy-Wuzzy, an'
          the missis and the kid;
        Our orders was to break you, an' of
          course we went an' did.
        We sloshed you with Martinis, an' it
          wasn't 'ardly fair;
        But for all the odds agin you, Fuzzy-
          Wuz, you bruk the square.

'E 'asn't got no papers of 'is own,
  'E 'asn't got no medals nor rewards,
So we must certify the skill 'e's shown
  In usin' of 'is long two-'anded swords;
When 'e's 'oppin' in an' out among the bush
  With 'is coffin-'eaded shield an' shovel-
    spear,
A 'appy day with Fuzzy on the rush
  Will last a 'ealthy Tommy for a year.

So 'ere's *to* you, Fuzzy-Wuzzy, **an'**
your friends which is no more,
If we 'adn't lost some messmates **we**
would 'elp you to deplore;
But give an' take's the gospel, **an'**
we'll call the bargain fair,
For if you 'ave lost more than **us,**
you crumpled up the square!

'E rushes at the smoke when we let drive,
An', before we know, 'e's 'ackin' at **our**
'ead;
'E's all 'ot sand an' ginger when alive,
An' 'e's generally shammin' when 'e's
dead.
'E's a daisy, 'e's a ducky, 'e's a lamb!
'E's a injia-rubber idiot on the spree,
'E's the on'y thing that doesn't care a **damn**
For the Regiment o' British Infantree.
So 'ere's *to* you, Fuzzy-Wuzzy, at **your**
'ome in the Sowdan;
You're a pore benighted 'eathen but **a**
first-class fightin' man;
An' 'ere's *to* you, Fuzzy-Fuzzy, **with**
your 'ayrick 'ead of 'air—
You big black boundin' beggar—**for**
you bruk a British square.

4

Oonts!

(*Northern India Transport Train.*)

WOT makes the soldier's 'eart to penk, wot
 . makes 'im to perspire?
It isn't standin' up to charge or lyin' down
  to fire ;
But it's everlastin' waitin' on a everlastin'
  road
For the commissariat camel an' 'is commis-
  sariat load.
    O the *oont*,[1] O the *oont*, O the commissa-
      riat *oont* !
    With 'is silly neck a-bobbin' like a
      basket full o' snakes ;
    We packs 'm like a idol, an' you ought
      to 'ear 'im grunt,
    An' when we gets 'im loaded up 'is
      blessed girth-rope breaks.

Wot makes the rear-guard swear so 'ard
  when night is drorin' in,
An' every native follower is shiverin' for 'is
  skin?

---

[1] Camel: *oo* is pronounced like *u* in "bull." but by Mr.
Atkins to rhyme with "front."

It ain't the chanst o' bein' rushed by Pay-
· thans frum the 'ills,
It's the commissariat camel puttin' on 'is
blessed frills !

    O the *oont*, O the *oont*, O the hairy scary
    oont !
    A-trippin' over tent-ropes when we've
    got the night alarm ;
    We socks 'im with a stretcher-pole an'
    'eads 'im off in front,
    An' when we've saved 'is bloomin' life
    'e chaws our bloomin' arm.

The 'orse 'e knows above a bit, the bullock's
but a fool,
The elephant's a gentleman, the baggage-
mule's a mule ;
But the commissariat cam-u-el, when all is
said an' done,
'E's a devil an' a ostrich an' a orphan-child
in one.

    O the *oont*, O the *oont*, O the Gawd-for-
    saken *oont !*
    The 'umpy-lumpy 'ummin'-bird a-sing-
    in' where 'e lies,
    'E's blocked the 'ole division from the
    rear-guard to the front,

An' when we gets 'im up again—the
  beggar goes an' dies !

'E'll gall an' chafe an' lame an' fight; 'e
  smells most awful vile ;
'E'll lose 'imself forever if you let 'im stray a
  mile ;
'E's game to graze the 'ole day long an' 'owl
  the 'ole night through,
An' when 'e comes to greasy ground 'e splits
  'isself in two.
    O the *oont*, O the *oont*, O the floppin',
      droppin' *oont !*
    When 'is long legs give from under an'
      'is meltin' eye is dim,
    The tribes is up be'ind us an' the tribes
      is out in front,
    It ain't no jam for Tommy, but it's kites
      and crows for 'im.

So when the cruel march is done an' when
  the roads is blind,
An' when we sees the camp in front an' 'ears
  the shots be'ind,
O then we strips 'is saddle off, and all 'is woes
  is past:
  E thinks on us that used 'im so, an' gets
  revenge at last.

O the *oont*, O the *oont*, O the floatin', bloatin' *oont !*
The late lamented camel in the water-cut he lies ;
We keeps a mile behind 'im an' we keeps a mile in front,
But 'e gets into the drinkin' casks, and then o' course we dies.

Loot.

IF you've ever stole a pheasant-egg be'ind
  the keeper's back,
  If you've ever snigged the washin' frum
    the line,
If you've ever crammed a gander in your
  bloomin' 'aversack,
  You will understand this little song o'
    mine.
But the service rules are 'ard, an' frum such
  we are debarred,
  For the same with British morals does not
    suit (*Cornet :* Toot! toot!)—
W'y, they call a man a robber if 'e stuffs 'is
  marchin' clobber
With the—
(*Chorus.*) Loo! loo! Lulu! lulu! Loo!
        loo! Loot! loot! loot!
        'Ow the loot!
        Bloomin' loot!
  That's the thing to make the boys git
    up an' shoot!

(54)

It's the same with dogs an' men,
If you'd make 'em come again
Clap 'em forward with a Loo! loo!
Lulu! Loot!
(*ff*) Whoopee! Tear 'im, puppy! Loo! loo!
Lulu! Loot! loot! loot!

If you've knocked a nigger edgeways when
'e's thrustin' for your life,
You must leave 'im very careful where 'e
fell;
An' may thank your stars an' gaiters if you
didn't feel 'is knife
That you ain't told off to bury him as
well.
Then the sweatin' Tommies wonder as they
spade the beggars under
Why lootin' should be entered as a crime;
So if my song you'll 'ear, I will learn you
plain an' clear
'Ow to pay yourself for fightin' overtime.
(*Chorus.*)   With the loot, etc.

Now remember when you're 'acking round
a gilded Burma god
That 'is eyes is very often precious stones;
An' if you treat a nigger to a dose o' cleanin'-
rod

'E's like to show you everything 'e owns.
When 'e won't prodooce no more, pour some
    water on the floor
  Where you 'ear it answer 'ollow to the
    boot (*Cornet:* Toot! toot!)—
When the ground begins to sink, shove your
    baynick down the chink,
  An' you're sure to touch the—
(*Chorus.*) Loo! loo! Lulu! Loot! loot!
      loot! .
        'Ow the loot, etc.

When from 'ouse to 'ouse you're 'untin' you
    must always work in pairs—
  It 'alves the gain, but safer you will find—
For a single man gits bottled on them twisty-
    wisty stairs,
  An' a woman comes and clobs 'im from
    be'ind.
When you've turned 'em inside out, an' it
    seems beyond a doubt
  As if there weren't enough to dust a flute
    (*Cornet:* Toot! toot!)—
Before you sling your 'ook, at the 'ouse-tops
    take a look,
  For it's underneath the tiles they 'ide the
    loot.
  (*Chorus.*) 'Ow the loot. etc.

You can mostly square a Sergint an' a Quar-
　　termaster too,
　　If you only take the proper way to go ;
I could never keep my pickin's, but I've
　　learned you all I knew—
　　An' don't you never say I told you so.
An' now I'll bid good-by, for I'm gettin'
　　rather dry,
　　An' I see another tunin' up to toot (*Cor-
net :* Toot ! toot !)—
So 'ere's good-luck to those that wears the
　　Widow's clo'es,
　　An' the Devil send 'em all they want o'
　　loot !
　　　　(*Chorus.*)　Yes, the loot,
　　　　　　　　　　Bloomin' loot.
　　In the tunic an' the mess-tin an' the
　　　　boot !
　　　　It's the same with dogs an' men,
　　　　If you'd make 'em come again
　　Whoop 'em forward with the Loo ! loo !
　　　　Lulu ! Loot ! loot ! loot !
　　Heeya ! Sick 'im, puppy ! Loo ! loo !
　　　　Lulu ! Loot ! loot ! loot !

Soldier, Soldier.

"SOLDIER, soldier come from the wars,
  Why don't you march with my true
    love?"
"We're fresh from off the ship, an' 'e's
    maybe give the slip,
  An' you'd best go look for a new love."
      New love! True love!
      Best go look for a new love,
      The dead they cannot rise, an' you'd bet-
        ter dry your eyes,
      An' you'd best go look for a new love.

"Soldier, soldier come from the wars,
  What did you see o' my true love?"
"I see 'im serve the Queen in a suit o' rifle-
    green,
  An' you'd best go look for a new love."

"Soldier, soldier come from the wars,
  Did ye see no more o' my true love?"
"I see 'im runnin' by when the shots begun
    to fly—
  But you'd best go look for a new love."

"Soldier, soldier come from the wars,
  Did aught take 'arm to my true love?"
"I couldn't see the fight, for the smoke it
    lay so white—
  An' you'd best go look for a new love."

"Soldier, soldier come from the wars,
  I'll **up** an' tend to my true love!"
" 'E's lying on the dead with a bullet through
    'is 'ead,
  An' you'd best go look for a new love."

"Soldier, soldier come from the wars,
  I'll lie down and die with my true love!"
"The pit we dug'll 'ide 'im an' twenty men
    beside 'im—
  An' you'd best go look for a new love."

"Soldier, soldier come from the wars,
  Do you bring no sign from my true love?"
"I bring a lock of 'air that 'e allus used to
    wear,
  An' you'd best go look for a new love."

"Soldier, soldier come from the wars,
  O then I know it's true I've lost my **true**
    love!"

" An' I tell you truth again—when you've
 lost the feel o' pain
You'd best take me for your true love."
  True love ! New love !
  Best take 'im for a new love.
  The dead they cannot rise, an' you'd
   better dry your eyes,
  An' you'd best take 'im for your true love.

The Sons of the Widow.

'AVE you 'eard o' the Widow at Windsor
 With a hairy gold crown on 'er 'ead ?
She 'as ships on the foam—she 'as millions
  at 'ome,
 An' she pays us poor beggars in red.
  (Ow, poor beggars in red !)
There's 'er nick on the cavalry 'orses
 There's 'er mark on the medical stores—
An' 'er troopers you'll find with a fair wind
  be'ind
That takes us to various wars.
  (Poor beggars !—barbarious wars !)
    Then 'ere's to the Widow at
      Windsor,
     An' 'ere's to the stores an' the
      guns,
    The men an' the 'orses what
      makes up the forces
    O' Missis Victorier's sons.
  (Poor beggars !—Victorier's sons !)

Walk wide o' the Widow at Windsor,
　For 'alf o' creation she owns:
We 'ave bought 'er the same with the sword
　　an' the flame,
　An we've salted it down with our bones.
　　　(Poor　beggars!—it's　blue　with　our
　　　bones!)
Hands off o' the sons of the Widow,
　Hands off o' the goods in 'er shop,
For the Kings must come down an' the
　. Emperors frown
When the Widow at Windsor says "Stop!"
　　　(Poor　beggars!—we're　sent　to　say
　　　'"Stop!")
　　　　　Then 'ere's to the Lodge o' the
　　　　　Widow,
　　　　　From the Pole to the Tropics
　　　　　it runs—
　　　　　To the Lodge that we tile with
　　　　　the rank an' the file,
　　　　　An' open in forms with the
　　　　　guns.
　　　(Poor　beggars!—it's　always　them
　　　guns!)

We 'ave 'eard o' the Widow at Windsor
　It's safest to let 'er alone:

For 'er sentries we stand by the sea an' the
    land
  Wherever the bugles are blown.
      (Poor beggars!—an' don't we get
      blown!)
Take 'old o' the wings o' the mornin',
  An' flop round the earth till you're dead;
But you won't get away from the tune that
    they play
  To the bloomin' old rag over'ead.
      (Poor beggars!—it's 'ot over'ead!)
        Then 'ere's to the sons o' the
        Widow,
        Wherever, 'owever they roam.
        'Ere's all they desire, an' if they
        require
        A speedy return to their 'ome.
      (Poor beggars!—they'll never see
  'ome!)

Troopin'.

(*Our Army in the East.*)

TROOPIN', troopin', troopin' to the sea :
'Ere's September come again—the six-year
   men are free.
O leave the dead be'ind us, for they cannot
   come away
To where the ship's a-coalin' up that takes
   us 'ome to-day.
     We're goin' 'ome, we're goin' 'ome,
     Our ship is *at* the shore,
     An' you must pack your 'aversack,
     For we won't come back no more.
     Ho, don't you grieve for me,
     My lovely Mary-Anne,
     For I'll marry you yit on a fourp'ny bit
     As a time-expired man.

The *Malabar's* in 'arbor with the *Jumner* at
   'er tail,
An' the time-expired's waitin' of 'is orders
   for to sail.

O the weary waitin' when on Khyber 'ills we
    lay,
But the time-expired's waitin' of 'is orders
    'ome to-day.

They'll turn us out at Portsmouth wharf in
    cold an' wet an' rain,
All wearin' Injian cotton kit, but we will not
    complain;
They'll kill us of pneumonia—for that's their
    little way—
But damn the chills and fever, men, we're
    goin' 'ome to-day!

Troopin', troopin'—winter's round again!
See the new draf's pourin' in for the old
    campaign;
Ho, you poor recruities, but you've got to
    earn your pay—
What's the last from Lunnon, lads? We're
    goin' there to-day.

Troopin', troopin', give another cheer—
'Ere's to English women an' a quart of Eng-
    lish beer;

The Colonel an' the regiment an' all who've
 got to stay,
Gawd's mercy strike 'em gentle—Whoop!
 we're goin' 'ome to-day.
  We're goin' 'ome, we're goin' 'ome,
  Our ship is *at* the shore,
  An' you must pack your 'aversack,
  For we won't come back no more.
  Ho, don't you grieve for me,
  My lovely Mary-Anne,
  For I'll marry you yit on a fourp'ny bit
  As a time-expired man.

Gunga Din.

THE *bhisti*, or water-carrier, attached to regiments in India, is often one of the most devoted of the Queen's servants. He is also appreciated by the men.

[THIS BALLAD IS EXTENSIVELY PLAGIARIZED.]

YOU may talk o' gin an' beer
When you're quartered safe out 'ere,
An' you're sent to penny-fights an' Alder-
shot it;
But if it comes to slaughter
You will do your work on water,
An' you'll lick the bloomin' boots of 'im
that's got it.
Now in Injia's sunny clime,
Where I used to spend my time
A-servin' of 'Er Majesty the Queen,
Of all them black-faced crew
The finest man I knew
Was our regimental *bhisti*, Gunga Din.
He was " Din! Din! Din!
You limping lump o' brick-dust, Gunga
Din!
Hi! *slippy hitherao!*
Water, get it! *Panee lao!*[1]
You squidgy-nosed old idol, Gunga Din!"

---

[1] Bring water swiftly.

The uniform 'e wore
Was nothin' much before,
An' rather less than 'arf o' that be'ind,
For a twisty piece o' rag
An' a goatskin water-bag
Was all the field-equipment 'e could find.
When the sweatin' troop-train lay
In a sidin' through the day,
Where the 'eat would make your bloomin'
   eyebrows crawl,
We shouted " Harry By !"[1]
Till our throats were bricky-dry,
Then we wopped 'im 'cause 'e couldn't serve
   us all.
   It was " Din ! Din ! Din !
   You 'eathen, where the mischief 'ave you
    been ?
   You put some *juldee* in it,
   Or I'll *marrow* you this minute[2]
   If you don't fill up my hemlet, Gunga
    Din !"

'E would dot 'an carry one
Till the longest day was done, .

---

[1] Mr. Atkins's equivalent for " O Brother !"
[2] Hit you.

An' 'e didn't seem to know the use o' fear.
If we charged or broke or cut,
You could bet your bloomin' nut, .
'E'd be waitin' fifty paces right flank rear.
With 'is *mussick* on 'is back,
'E would skip with our attack,
An' watch us till the bugles made " Retire;"
An' for all 'is dirty 'ide
'E was white, clear white, inside
When 'e went to tend the wounded under
    fire !
    It was " Din ! Din ! Din !"
    With the bullets kickin' dust-spots on the
       green.
    When the cartridges ran out,
    You could 'ear the front-files shout:
    "Hi! ammunition-mules an' Gunga
       Din !"

I sha'n't forgit the night
When I dropped be'ind the fight
With a bullet where my belt-plate should
    'a' been.
I was chokin' mad with thirst,
An' the man that spied me first
Was our good old grinnin', gruntin' Gunga
    Din.

'E lifted up my 'ead,
An' 'e plugged me where I bled,
An' 'e guv me 'arf-a-pint o' water—green:
It was crawlin' and it stunk,
But of all the drinks I've drunk,
I'm gratefullest to one from Gunga Din.
  It was " Din! Din! Din!
  'Ere's a beggar with a bullet through 'is
      spleen;
  'E's chawin' up the ground an' 'e's kickin'
      all around:
  For Gawd's sake git the water, Gunga
      Din!"

'E carried me away
To where a *dooli* lay,
An' a bullet come an' drilled the beggar
    clean;
'E put me safe inside,
An' just before 'e died,
" I 'ope you liked your drink," sez Gunga
    Din.
So I'll meet 'im later on
In the place where 'e is gone—
Where it's always double drill and no can-
    teen;

'E'll be squattin' on the coals
Givin' drink to pore damned souls,
An' I'll get a swig in Hell from Gunga
  Din !.
    Din ! Din ! Din !
    You Lazarushian-leather Gunga Din !
    Tho' I've belted you an' flayed you,
    By the livin' Gawd that made you,
    You're a better man than I am, Gunga
      Din !

Mandaiay.

BY the old Moulmein Pagoda, lookin' east-
ward to the sea,
There's a Burma girl a-settin', an' I know
she thinks o' me;
For the wind is in the palm-trees, an' the
temple-bells they say,
"Come you back, you British soldier; come
you back to Mandalay!"
    Come you back to Mandalay,
    Where the old Flotilla lay;
    Can't you 'ear their paddles chunkin'
      from Rangoon to Mandalay?
    O the road to Mandalay,
    Where the flyin'-nshes play,
    An' the dawn comes up like thunder
    outer China 'crost the Bay!

'Er petticut was yaller an' 'er little cap was
green,
An' 'er name was Supi-yaw-lat—jes' the
same as Theebaw's Queen,

An' I seed her fust a-smokin' of a whackin'
    white cheroot,
An' a-wastin' Christian kisses on an 'eathen
    idol's foot:
      Bloomin' idol made o' mud—
      Wot they called the Great Gawd Budd—
      Plucky lot she cared for idols when I
        kissed 'er where she stud !
      On the road to Mandalay—

When the mist was on the rice-fields an' the
    sun was droppin' slow,
She'd git 'er little banjo an' she'd sing
 " *Kulla-lo-lo !*"
With 'er arm upon my shoulder an' her
    cheek agin my cheek
We useter watch the steamers an' the *hathis*
    pilin' teak.
      Elephints a-pilin' teak
      In the sludgy, squdgy creek,
      Where the silence 'ung that 'eavy you
        was 'arf afraid to speak !
      On the road to Mandalay—

But that's all shove be'ind me—long ago an'
    fur away,
An' there ain't no 'buses runnin' from the
    Benk to Mandalay ;

An' I'm learnin' 'ere in London what the
   ten-year sodger tells:
" If you've 'eard the East a-callin', why, you
   won't 'eed nothin' else."
     No ! you won't 'eed nothin' else
     But them spicy garlic smells
     An' the sunshine and the palm-trees an'
       the tinkly temple-bells !
     On the road to Mandalay—

I am sick o' wastin' leather on these gutty
   pavin'-stones,
An' the blasted Henglish drizzle wakes the
   fever in my bones ;
Tho' I walks with fifty 'ousemaids outer
   Chelsea to the Strand,
An' they talks a lot o' lovin', but wot do
   they understand ?
     Beefy face an' grubby 'and—
     Law ! wot *do* they understand ?
     I've a neater, sweeter maiden in a
      cleaner, greener land !
     On the road to Mandalay—

Ship me somewheres east of Suez where the
   best is like the worst,
Where there aren't no Ten Commandments,
   an' a man can raise a thirst ;

For the temple-bells are callin', an' it's there
   that I would be—
By the old Moulmein Pagoda, lookin' lazy
   at the sea—
     On the road to Mandalay,
     Where the old Flotilla lay,
     With our sick beneath the awnings
      when we went to Mandalay !
     Oh, the road to Mandalay,
     Where the flyin'-fishes play,
     An' the dawn comes up like thunder
      outer China 'crost the Bay

The Young British Soldier.

WHEN the 'arf-made recruity goes out to
  the East
'E acts like a babe an' 'e drinks like a beast,
An' 'e wonders because 'e is frequent de-
  ceased
    Ere 'e's fit for to serve as a soldier.
      Serve, serve, serve as a soldier,
      Serve, serve, serve as a soldier,
      Serve, serve, serve as a soldier,
        So-oldier *hof* the Queen !

Now all you recruities what's drafted to-day,
You shut up your rag-box an' 'ark to my lay,
An' I'll sing you a soldier as far as I may :
    A soldier what's fit for a soldier.
      Fit, fit, fit for a soldier—

First, mind you steer clear o' the grog-sellers'
  huts,
For they sell you Fixed Bay'nets that rots
  out your guts—

A drink that 'ud eat the live steel from your
   butts—
     An' it's bad for the young British soldier.
     Bad, bad, bad for the soldier—

When the cholera comes—as it will past a
   doubt—
Keep out of the wet and don't go on the
   shout,
For the sickness comes in as the liquor dies
   out,
     An' it crumples the young British soldier.
     Crum-, crum-, crumples the soldier—

But the worst o' your foes is the sun over'ead;
You *must* wear your 'elmet for all that is said.
If 'e finds you uncovered 'e'll knock you
   down dead,
     An' you'll die like a fool of a soldier.
     Fool, fool, fool of a soldier—

If you're cast for fatigue by a sergeant unkind,
Don't grouse like a woman nor crack on nor
   blind;
Be handy and civil, and then you will find
     As it's beer for the young British soldier.
     Beer, beer, beer for the soldier—

Now, if you must marry, take care she is old—
A troop-sergeant's widow's the nicest I'm
    told—
For beauty won't help if your vittles is
    cold,
      An' love ain't enough for a soldier.
        'Nough, 'nough, 'nough for a soldier—

If the wife should go wrong with a comrade,
    be loath
To shoot when you catch 'em—you'll swing,
    on my oath !—
Make 'im take 'er and keep 'er; that's hell
    for them both,
      An' you're quit o' the curse of a soldier.
        Curse, curse, curse of a soldier—

When first under fire an' you're wishful to
    duck,
Don't look or take 'eed at the man that is
    struck,
Be thankful you're livin' an' trust to your
    luck,
      An' march to your front like a soldier.
        Front, front, front like a soldier.

When 'arf of your bullets fly wide in the
    ditch,
Don't call your Martini a cross-eyed old
    bitch ;
She's human as your are—you treat her as
    sich,
      An' she'll fight for the young British
        soldier.
      Fight, fight, fight for the soldier—

When shakin' their bustles like ladies so fine
The guns o' the enemy wheel into line ;
Shoot low at the limbers and don't mind the
    shine,
      For noise never startles the soldier.
      Start-, start-, startles the soldier—

If your officer's dead and the sergeants look
    white,
Remember it's ruin to run from a fight ;
So take open order, lie down, and sit tight,
      An' wait for supports like a soldier.
      Wait, wait, wait like a soldier—

When you're wounded an' left on Afghanis-
    tan's plains,
An' the women come out to cut up your
    remains,

Jest roll to your rifle an' blow out **your**
  brains,
    An' go to your Gawd like a soldier:
      Go, go, go like a soldier,
      Go, go, go like a soldier,
      Go, go, go like a soldier,
        So-oldier *hof* the Queen.

Screw-Guns.

SMOKIN' my pipe on the mountings, sniffin'
   the mornin'-cool,
I walks in my old brown gaiters along o' my
   old brown mule,
With seventy gunners be'ind me, an' never
   a beggar forgets
It's only the pick o' the Army that handles
   the dear little pets—Tss! Tss!
     For you all love the screw-guns—the
       screw-guns they all love you.
     So when we call round with a few guns,
       o' course you will know what to do—
       hoo! hoo!
     Jest send in your Chief an' surrender—
       it's worse if you fights or you runs:
     You can go where you please, you can
       skid up the trees, but you don't get
       away from the guns.

They send us along where the roads are, but
    mostly we goes where they ain't;
We'd climb up the side of a sign-board, an'
    trust to the stick o' the paint;

We've chivied the Naga an' Lushai, we've
    give the Afreedeeman fits,
For we fancies ourselves at two thousand,
    we guns that are built in two bits—Tss!
Tss!
      For you all love the screw-guns—

If a man doesn't work, why, we drills 'im
    an' teaches 'im 'ow to be'ave;
If a beggar can't march, why, we kills 'im
    an' rattles 'im into 'is grave.
You've got to stand up to our business an'
    spring without snatchin' or fuss.
D' you say that you sweat with the field-
    guns? By God, you must lather with us—
Tss! Tss!
      For you all love the screw-guns—

The eagles is screamin' around us, the
    river's a-moanin' below,
We're clear o' the pine an' the oak-scrub,
    we're out on the rocks an' the snow,
An' the wind is as thin as a whip-lash what
    carries away to the plains
The rattle an' stamp o' the lead-mules—the
    jinglety-jink o' the chains—Tss! Tss!
      For you all love the screw-guns—

There's a wheel on the Horns o' the Mornin,
   an' a wheel on the edge o' the Pit,
An' a drop into nothin' beneath us as straight
   as a beggar can spit;
With the sweat runnin' out o' your shirt-
   sleeves an' the sun off the snow in your
   face,
An' 'arf o' the men on the drag-ropes to
   hold the old gun in 'er place—Tss! Tss!
   For you all love the screw-guns—

Smokin' my pipe on the mountings, sniffin'
   the mornin'-cool,
I climbs in my old brown gaiters along o'
   my old brown mule.
The monkey can say what our road was—
   the wild-goat 'e knows where we passed.
Stand easy, you long-eared old darlin's!
   Out drag-ropes! With shrapnel! Hold
   fast!—Tss! Tss!

   For you all love the screw-guns—the
     screw-guns they all love you!
   So when we take tea with a few guns,
     o' course you will know what to do—
     hoo! hoo!

Just send in your Chief and surrender—
  it's worse if you fights or you runs:
You may hide in the caves, they'll be
  only your graves, but you don't get
  away from the guns!

Belts.

THERE was a row in Silver Street that's
    near to Dublin Quay,
Between an Irish regiment an' English cav-
    alree;
It started at Revelly an' it lasted on till
    dark;
The first man dropped at Harrison's, the last
    forninst the Park.
      For it was "Belts, belts, belts, an' that's
        one for you!"
      An' it was "Belts, belts, belts, an' that's
        done for you!"
      O buckle an' tongue
      Was the song that we sung
      From Harrison's on to the Park!

There was a row in Silver Street—the regi-
    ments was out,
They called us "Delhi Rebels," an' we an-
    swered "Threes about!"

That drew them like a hornet's nest—we
　met them good an' large,
The English at the double an' the Irish at
　the charge.
　　Then it was: Belts—

There was a row in Silver Street—an' I was
　in it too ;
We passed the time o' day, an' then the belts
　went *whirraru ;*
I misremember what occurred, but subse-
　quint the storm
A *Freeman's Journal Supplemint* was all my
　uniform.
　　O it was: Belts—

There was a row in Silver Street—they sent
　the Polis there,
The English were too drunk to know, the
　Irish didn't care ;
But when they grew impertinent we simul-
　taneous rose,
Till half o' them was Liffey mud an' half
　was tatthered clo'es.
　　For it was: Belts—

There was a row in Silver Street—it might
  ha' raged till now,
But some one drew his side-arm clear, an'
  nobody knew how;
'Twas Hogan took the point an' dropped;
  we saw the red blood run:
An' so we all was murderers that started out
  in fun.
  While it was: Belts—

There was a row in Silver Street—but that
  took off the shine,
Wid each man whishperin' to his next:
  " 'Twas never work o' mine!"
We went away like beaten dogs, an' down
  the street we bore him,
The poor dumb corpse that couldn't see the
  bhoys were sorry for him.
  When it was: Belts—

There was a row in Silver Street—it isn't
  over yet,
For half of us are under guard wid pun-
  ishmints to get;
'Tis all a mericle to me as in the Clink I lie;
There was a row in Silver Street—begod, I
  wonder why!

But it was " Belts, belts, belts, an' that's
    one for you !"
An' it was " Belts, belts, belts, an' that's
    done for you !"
O buckle an' tongue
Was the song that we sung
From Harrison's down to the Park !

To the Unknown Goddess.

WILL you conquer my heart with your
    beauty ; my soul going out from afar?
Shall I fall to your hand as a victim of
    crafty and cautious *shikar ?*

Have I met you and passed you already,
    unknowing, unthinking, and blind ?
Shall I meet you next session at Simla, O
    sweetest and best of your kind ?

Does the P. and O. bear you to me-ward, or,
    clad in short frocks in the West,
Are you growing the charms that shall cap-
    ture and torture the heart in my breast ?

Will you stay in the Plains till September—
    my passion as warm as the day ?
Will you bring me to book on the Moun-
    tains, or where the thermantidotes play ?

When the light of your eyes shall make
    pallid the mean lesser lights I pursue,
And the charm of your presence shall lure
    me from love of the gay " thirteen-two ;"

When the peg and the pig-skin shall please
 not; when I buy me Calcutta-built
 clothes ;
When I quit the Delight of Wild Asses ; for-
 swearing the swearing of oaths;

As a deer to the hand of the hunter when I
 turn 'mid the gibes of my friends ;
When the days of my freedom are num-
 bered, and the life of the bachelor ends.

Ah Goddess ! child, spinster, or widow—as
 of old on Mars Hill when they raised
To the God that they knew not an altar—so
 I, a young Pagan, have praised

The Goddess I know not nor worship; yet,
 if half that men tell me be true,
You will come in the future, and therefore
 these verses are written to you.

La Nuit Blanche.

A MUCH-DISCERNING Public hold
The Singer generally sings
Of personal and private things,
And prints and sells his past for gold.

Whatever I may here disclaim,
The very clever folk I sing to
Will most indubitably cling to
Their pet delusion, just the same.

I HAD seen, as dawn was breaking
And I staggered to my rest,
Tari Devi softly shaking
From the Cart Road to the crest.
I had seen the spurs of Jakko
Heave and quiver, swell and sink.
Was it Earthquake or tobacco,
Day of Doom or Night of Drink?

In the full, fresh, fragrant morning
I observed a camel crawl,
Laws of gravitation scorning,
On the ceiling and the wall;
Then I watched a fender walking,
And I heard gray leeches sing,
And a red-hot monkey talking
Did not seem the proper thing.

Then a Creature, skinned and crimson,
    Ran about the floor and cried,
And they said I had the "jims" on,
    And they dosed me with bromide,
And they locked me in my bedroom—
    Me and one wee Blood Red Mouse—
Though I said : " To give my head room
    " You bad best unroof the house."

But my words were all unheeded,
    Though I told the grave M.D.
That the treatment really needed
    Was a dip in open sea
That was lapping just below me,
    Smooth as silver, white as snow,
And it took three men to throw me
    When I found I could not go.

Half the night I watched the Heavens
    Fizz like '81 champagne—
Fly to sixes and to sevens,
    Wheel and thunder back again;
And when all was peace and order
    Save one planet nailed askew,
Much I wept because my warder
    Would not let me set it true.

After frenzied hours of waiting,
   When the Earth and Skies were **dumb**,
Pealed an awful voice dictating
   An interminable sum,
Changing to a tangled story—
   " What she said you said I said—"
Till the Moon arose in glory,
   And I found her . . . in my head;

Then a Face came blind and weeping,
   And It couldn't wipe Its eyes,
And It muttered I was keeping
   Back the moonlight from the skies;
So I patted it for pity,
   But It whistled shrill with wrath,
And a hugh black Devil City
   Poured its peoples on my path.

So I fled with steps uncertain
   On a thousand-year long race,
But the bellying of the curtain
   Kept me always in one place;
While the tumult rose and maddened
   To the roar of Earth on fire,
Ere it ebbed and sank and saddened
   To a whisper tense as wire.

In intolerable stillness
   Rose one little, little star,
And it chuckled at my illness,
   And it mocked me from afar;
And its brethren came and eyed me,
   Called the Universe to aid,
Till I lay with naught to hide me,
   'Neath the Scorn of All Things Made.

Dun and saffron, robed and splendid,
   Broke the solemn, pitying Day,
And I knew my pains were ended,
   And I turned and tried to pray;
But my speech was shattered wholly,
   And I wept as children weep,
Till the dawn-wind, softly, slowly,
   Brought to burning eyelids sleep.

My Rival.

I GO to concert, party, ball—
    What profit is in these ?
I sit alone against the wall
    And strive to look at ease.
The incense that is mine by right
    They burn before Her shrine;
And that's because I'm seventeen
    And She is forty-nine.

I cannot check my girlish blush,
    My color comes and goes;
I redden to my finger-tips,
    And sometimes to my nose.
But she is white where white should be,
    And red where red should shine.
The blush that flies at seventeen
    Is fixed at forty-nine.

I wish *I* had Her constant cheek:
    I wish that I could sing
All sorts of funny little songs,
    Not quite the proper thing.

I'm very *gauche* and very shy,
  Her jokes aren't in my line;
And, worst of all, I'm seventeen
  While She is forty-nine.

The young men come, the young men go,
  Each pink and white and neat,
She's older than their mothers, but
  They grovel at Her feet.
They walk beside Her 'rickshaw wheels—
  None ever walk by mine;
And that's because I'm seventeen
  And She is forty-nine.

She rides with half a dozen men,
  (She calls them " boys " and " mashers ")
I trot along the Mall alone;
  My prettiest frocks and sashes
Don't help to fill my programme-card,
  And vainly I repine
From ten to two A.M.   Ah me!
  Would I were forty-nine!

She calls me " darling," " pet," and " dear,"
  And " sweet retiring maid."
I'm always at the back, I know,
  She puts me in the shade.

She introduces me to men,
  "Cast" lovers, I opine,
For sixty takes to seventeen,
  Nineteen to forty-nine.

But even she must older grow
  And end her dancing days,
She can't go on forever so
  At concerts, balls, and plays.
One ray of priceless hope I see
  Before my footsteps shine;
Just think, that She'll be eighty-one
  When I am forty-nine.

The Lovers' Litany.

EYES of gray—a sodden quay,
Driving rain and falling tears,
As the steamer wears to sea
In a parting storm of cheers.
   Sing, for Faith and Hope are high—
   None so true as you and I—
   Sing the Lovers' Litany :—
   " Love like ours can never die !"

Eyes of black—a throbbing keel,
Milky foam to left and right;
Whispered converse near the wheel
In the brilliant tropic night.
   Cross that rules the Southern Sky!
   Stars that sweep and wheel and fly,
   Hear the Lovers' Litany :—
   " Love like ours can never die !"

Eyes of brown—a dusty plain
Split and parched with heat of June,
Flying hoof and tightened rein,
Hearts that beat the old, old tune.

Side by side the horses fly,
Frame we now the old reply
Of the Lovers' Litany :—
" *Love like ours can never die !*"

Eyes of blue—the Simla Hills
Silvered with the moonlight hoar;
Pleading of the waltz that thrills,
Dies and echoes round Benmore.
 " *Mabel,*" "*Officers,*" " *Good-by,*"
Glamour, wine, and witchery—
On my soul's sincerity,
" *Love like ours can never die !*"

Maidens, of your charity,
Pity my most luckless state.
Four times Cupid's debtor I—
Bankrupt in quadruplicate.
 Yet, despite this evil case,
 An a maiden showed me grace,
Four-and-forty times would I
Sing the Lovers' Litany :—
" *Love like ours can never die !*"

A Ballad of Burial.

(*"Saint Praxed's ever was the Church for peace."*)

IF down here I chance to die,
  Solemnly I beg you take
All that is left of " I,"
  To the Hills for old sake's sake.
Pack me very thoroughly
  In the ice that used to slake
Pegs I drank when I was dry—
  This observe for old sake's sake.

To the railway station hie,
  There a single ticket take
For Umballa—goods-train—I
  Shall not mind delay or shake.
I shall rest contentedly
  Spite of clamor coolies make;
Thus in state and dignity
  Send me up for old sake's sake.

Next the sleepy Babu wake,
  Book a Kalka van " for four."
Few, I think, will care to make
  Journeys with me any more

As they used to do of yore.
  I shall need a " special " break—
Thing I never took before—
  Get me one for old sake's sake.

After that—arrangements make.
  No hotel will take me in,
And a bullock's back would break
  'Neath the teak and leaden skin.
Tonga ropes are frail and thin,
  Or, did I a back-seat take,
In a tonga I might spin,—
  Do your best for old sake's sake.

After that—your work is done.
  Recollect a Padre must
Mourn the dear departed one—
  Throw the ashes and the dust.
Don't go down at once.   I trust
  You will find excuse to " snake
Three days' casual on the bust,"
  Get your fun for old sake's sake.

I could never stand the Plains.
  Think of blazing June and May,
Think of those September rains
  Yearly till the Judgment Day!

I should never rest in peace,
    I should sweat and lie awake.
Rail me then, on my decease,
    To the Hills for old sake's sake.

Divided Destinies.

IT was an artless *Bandar*, and he danced
    upon a pine,
And much I wondered how he lived, and
    where the beast might dine,
And many, many other things, till, o'er my
    morning smoke,
I slept the sleep of idleness and dreamt that
    Bandar spoke.

He said: "O man of many clothes! Sad
    crawler on the Hills !
Observe, I know not Ranken's shop, nor
    Ranken's monthly bills ;
I take no heed to trousers or the coats that
    you call dress ;
Nor am I plagued with little cards for little
    drinks at Mess.

"I steal the bunnia's grain at morn, at noon
    and eventide,
(For he is fat and I am spare), I roam the
    mountain side,

I follow no man's carriage, and no, never **in**
    my life
Have I flirted at Peliti's with another *Ban-*
    dar's wife.

"O man of futile fopperies—unnecessary
    wraps;
I own no ponies in the hills, I drive no tall-
    wheeled traps;
I buy me not twelve-button gloves, ' short-
    sixes ' eke, or rings,
Nor do I waste at Hamilton's my wealth on
    ' pretty things.'

"I quarrel with my wife at home, we never
    fight abroad;
But Mrs. B. has grasped the fact I am her
    only lord.
I never heard of fever—dumps nor debts de-
    press my soul;
And I pity and despise you!" Here he
    pouched my breakfast-roll.

His hide was very mangy, and his face was
    very red,
And ever and anon he scratched with en-
    ergy his head.

His manners were not always nice, but how
  my spirit cried
To be an artless *Bandar* loose upon the
  mountain side!

So I answered: " Gentle *Bandar*, an inscru-
  table Decree ⋅
Makes thee a gleesome fleasome Thou, and
  me a wretched Me.
Go! Depart in peace, my brother, to thy
  home amid the pine;
Yet forget not once a mortal wished to
  change his lot with thine."

The Masque of Plenty.

ARGUMENT.—The Indian Government, being minded to discover the economic condition of their lands, sent a Committee to inquire into it; and saw that it was good.

SCENE.—*The wooded heights of Simla. The Incarnation of the Government of India in the raiment of the Angel of Plenty sings, to pianoforte accompaniment :—*

" HOW sweet is the shepherd's sweet life !
From the dawn to the even he strays—
He shall follow his sheep all the day,
   And his tongue shall be filled with praise

(*Adagio dim.*) Filled with praise !"

(*Largendo con sp.*) Now this is the position,
     Go make an inquisition
     Into their real condition
     As swiftly as ye may.

(*p.*) Ay, paint our swarthy billions
    The richest of vermilions
    Ere two well-led cotillions
    Have danced themselves away.

Turkish Patrol, *as able and intelligent Investigators wind down the Himalayas :—*

What is the state. of the Nation? What is
   its occupation?
Hi! get along, get along, get along—lend us
   the information!

(*Dim.*) Census the *byle* and the *yabu*—capture a first-class Babu,
Set him to cut Gazetteers—Gazetteers . . .
   (*ff.*) What is the state of the Nation,
   etc., etc.

Interlude, *from Nowhere in Particular, to stringed and Oriental instruments.*

Our cattle reel beneath the yoke they bear—
   The earth is iron, and the skies are brass—
And faint with fervor of the naming air
   The languid hours pass.

The well is dry beneath the village tree—
   The young wheat withers ere it reach a
   span,
And belts of blinding sand show cruelly
   Where once the river ran.

Pray, brothers, pray, but to no earthly King—
  Lift up your hands above the blighted
    grain,
Look westward—if they please, the Gods
    shall bring
  Their mercy with the rain.

Look westward—bears the blue no brown
    cloud-bank?
  Nay, it is written—wherefore should we
    fly?
On our own field and by our cattle's flank
  Lie down, lie down to die!

Semi-Chorus.

By the plumed heads of Kings
            Waving high,
Where the tall corn springs
            O'er the dead.

If they rust or rot we die,
If they ripen we are fed.
Very mighty is the power of our Kings!

*Triumphal return to Simla of the Investigators,
attired after the manner of Dionysus, lead-
ing a pet tiger-cub in wreaths of rhubarb
leaves, symbolical of India under medical
treatment. They sing :—*

We have seen, we have written—behold it,
    the proof of our manifold toil!
In their hosts they assembled and told it—
    the tale of the sons of the soil.
We have said of the Sickness, "Where is
    it?"—and of Death, "It is far from our
    ken;"
We have paid a particular visit to the afflu-
    ent children of men.
We have trodden the mart and the well-
    curb—we have stooped to the bield and
    the byre;
And the King may the forces of Hell curb,
    for the people have all they desire!

Castanets and step-dance :

Oh, the *dom* and the *mag* and the *thakur* and
    the *thag*,
    And the *nat* and the *brinjaree*,
And the *bunnia* and the *ryot* are as happy
    and as quiet
    And as plump as they can be!

Yes, the *jain* and the *jat* in his stucco-fronted
 hut,
  And the bounding *bazugar,*
By the favor of the King, are as fat as any-
 thing,
  They are—they are—they are !

RECITATIVE, *Government of India, with white
 satin wings and electroplated harp :—*

How beautiful upon the mountains—in
 peace reclining,
Thus to be assured that our people are unani-
 mously dining.
And though there are places not so blessed
 as others in natural advantages, which,
 after all, was only to be expected,
Proud and glad are we to congratulate you
 upon the work you have thus ably effected.
(*Cres.*) How be-ewtiful upon the mountains !

HIRED BAND, *brasses only, full chorus :—*

  God bless the Squire
  And all his rich relations
  Who teach us poor people
  We eat our proper rations—

We eat our proper rations,
In spite of inundations,
Malarial exhalations,
And casual starvations,
We have, we have, they say we have—
We *have* our proper rations !

(*Cornet.*)

Which nobody can deny !
If he does he tells a lie—
  We are all as willing as Barkis—
  We all of us loves the Markiss—
  We all of us stuffs our ca-ar-kis—
With food until we die ! (*Da capo.*)

CHORUS OF THE CRYSTALLIZED FACTS.

Before the beginning of years
There came to the rule of the State
Men with a pair of shears,
Men with an Estimate—
Strachey with Muir for leaven,
Lytton with locks that fell,
Ripon fooling with Heaven,
And Temple riding like H-ll !

And the bigots took in hand
Cess and the falling of rain,
And the measure of sifted sand
The dealer puts in the grain—
Imports by land and sea,
To uttermost decimal worth,
And registration—free—
In the houses of death and of birth:
And fashioned with pens and paper,
And fashioned in black and white,
With Life for a flickering taper
And Death for a blazing light—
With the Armed and the Civil Power,
That his strength might endure for a
   span,
From Adam's Bridge to Peshawur,
The Much Administered man.

In the towns of the North and the East,
They gathered us unto rule,
They bade him starve the priest
And send his children to school.
Railways and roads they wrought,
For the needs of the soil within;
A time to squabble in court,
A time to bear and to grin.

And gave him peace in his ways,
Jails—and Police to fight,
Justice at length of days,
And Right—and Might in the **Right**.
His speech is of mortgaged bedding,
On his kine he borrows yet,
At his heart is his daughter's wedding,
In his eye foreknowledge of debt.
He eats and hath indigestion,
He toils and he may not stop;
His life is a long-drawn question
Between a crop and a crop.

The Mare's Nest.

JANE Austen Beecher Stowe de Rouse
  Was good beyond all earthly need;
But, on the other hand, her spouse
  Was very, very bad indeed.
He smoked cigars, called churches slow,
And raced—but this she did not know.

For Belial Machiavelli kept
  The little fact a secret, and,
Though o'er his minor sins she wept,
  Jane Austen did not understand
That Lilly—thirteen-two and bay,—
Absorbed one-half her husband's pay.

She was so good, she made him worse;
  (Some women are like this, I think;)
He taught her parrot how to curse,
  Her Assam monkey how to drink.
He vexed her righteous soul until
She went up, and he went down hill.

Then came the crisis, strange to say,
　　Which turned a good wife to a better.
A telegraphic peon, one day,
　　Brought her—now, had it been a letter
For Belial Machiavelli, I
Know Jane would just have let it lie.

But 'twas a telegram instead,
　　Marked " urgent," and her duty plain
To open it.　Jane Austen read:—
　　" Your Lilly's got a cough again.
Can't understand why she is kept
At your expense."　Jane Austin wept.

It was a misdirected wire.
　　Her husband was at Shaitanpore.
She spread her anger, hot as fire,
　　Through six thin foreign sheets or **more,**
Sent off that letter, wrote another
To her solicitor—and mother.

Then Belial Machiavelli saw
　　Her error and, I trust, his own,
Wired to the minion of the Law,
　　And travelled wifeward—not alone.
For Lilly—thirteen-two and bay—
Came in a horse-box all the way.

There was a scene—a weep or two—
  With many kisses. Austen Jane
Rode Lilly all the season through,
  And never opened wires again.
She races now with Belial. This
Is very sad, but so it is.

Christmas in India.

DIM dawn behind the tamarisks—the sky is
   saffron-yellow—
As the women in the village grind the
   corn,
And the parrots seek the river-side, each
   calling to his fellow
That the Day, the staring Eastern Day is
   born.
   Oh the white dust on the highway! Oh
      the stenches in the byway!
   Oh the clammy fog that hovers over
      earth!
   And at Home they're making merry
      'neath the white and scarlet berry—
   What part have India's exiles in their
      mirth?

Full day behind the tamarisks—the sky is
   blue and staring—
As the cattle crawl afield beneath the
   yoke,

And they bear One o'er the field-path, who
　　is past all hope or caring,
　To the ghat below the curling wreaths of
　　　smoke.
　　　Call on Rama, going slowly, as ye bear
　　　　a brother lowly—
　　　　Call on Rama—he may hear, perhaps,
　　　　　your voice!
　　　With our hymn-books and our psalters
　　　　we appeal to other altars,
　　　　And to-day we bid "good Christian
　　　　　men rejoice!"

High noon behind the tamarisks—the sun
　　is hot above us—
　As at Home the Christmas Day is break-
　　　ing wan.
They will drink our healths at dinner—those
　　who tell us how they love us,
　And forget us till another year be gone!
　　　Oh the toil that needs no breaking! Oh
　　　　the *Heimweh*, ceaseless, aching!
　　　　Oh the black dividing Sea and alien
　　　　　Plain!
　　　Youth was cheap—wherefore we sold it.
　　　　Gold was good—we hoped to hold it,
　　　　And to-day we know the fulness of
　　　　　our gain.

Gray dusk behind the tamarisks—the par-
    rots fly together—
As the sun is sinking slowly over Home;
And his last ray seems to mock us shackled
    in a lifelong tether
That drags us back howe'er so far we
    roam.
    Hard her service, poor her payment—
        she in ancient, tattered raiment—
      India, she the grim Stepmother of
      our kind.
    If a year of life be lent her, if her tem-
        ple's shrine we enter,
      The door is shut—we may not look
      behind.

Black night behind the tamarisks—the owls
    begin their chorus—
As the conches from the temple scream
    and bray.
With the fruitless years behind us, and the
    hopeless years before us,
    Let us honor, O my brothers, Christmas
    Day!
    Call a truce, then, to our labors—let us
        feast with friends and neighbors,
      And be merry as the custom of our
      caste;

For if " faint and forced the laughter,'
    and if sadness follow after,
  We are richer by one mocking Christ-
    mas past.

Pagett, M.P.

THE toad beneath the harrow knows
Exactly where each tooth-point goes.
The butterfly upon the road
Preaches contentment to that toad.

PAGETT, M.P., was a liar, and a fluent liar
therewith,—
He spoke of the heat of India as the "Asian
Solar Myth;"
Came on a four months' visit, to "study the
East," in November,
And I got him to sign an agreement vowing
to stay till September.

March came in with the *köil*. Pagett was
cool and gay,
Called me a "bloated Brahmin," talked of
my "princely pay."
March went out with the roses. "Where is
your heat?" said he.
"Coming," said I to Pagett. "Skittles!"
said Pagett, M.P.

(121)

April began with the punkah, coolies, and
   prickly-heat,—
Pagett was dear to mosquitoes, sandflies
   found him a treat.
He grew speckled and lumpy—hammered,
   I grieve to say,
Aryan brothers who fanned him, in an il-
   liberal way.

May set in with a dust-storm,—Pagett went
   down with the sun.
All the delights of the season tickled him
   one by one.
Imprimis—ten days' "liver"—due to his
   drinking beer ;
Later, a dose of fever—slight, but he called
   it severe.

Dysent'ry touched him in June, after the
   Chota Bursat—
Lowered his portly person—made him yearn
   to depart.
He didn't call me a " Brahmin," or " bloat-
   ed," or " overpaid,"
But seemed to think it a wonder that any
   one stayed.

July was a trifle unhealthy,—Pagett was ill
    with fear,
'Called it the " Cholera Morbus," hinted that
    life was dear.
He babbled of "Eastern exile," and men-
    tioned his home with tears ;
But I hadn't seen *my* children for close upon
    seven years.

We reached a hundred and twenty once in
    the Court at noon,
(I've mentioned Pagett was portly) Pagett
    went off in a swoon.
That was an end to the business ; Pagett, the
    perjured, fled
With a practical, working knowledge of
    " Solar Myths " in his head.

And I laughed as I drove from the station,
    but the mirth died out on my lips
As I thought of the fools like Pagett who
    write of their " Eastern trips,"
And the sneers of the travelled idiots who
    duly misgovern the land,
And I prayed to the Lord to deliver another
    one into my hand.

The Song of the Women.

(Lady Dufferin's Fund for medical aid to the Women of India.)

HOW shall she know the worship we would
    do her?
The walls are high, and she is very far.
How shall the women's message reach unto
    her
    Above the tumult of the packed bazaar?
        Free wind of March, against the lattice
          blowing,
        Bear thou our thanks, lest she depart
          unknowing.

Go forth across the fields we may not roam
    in,
    Go forth beyond the trees that rim the
      city,
To whatsoe'er fair place she hath her home
    in,
    Who dowered us with wealth of love and
      pity.

Out of our shadow pass, and seek her
    singing—
"I have no gifts but Love alone for
    bringing."

Say that we be a feeble folk who greet her,
  But old in grief, and very wise in tears;
Say that we, being desolate, entreat her
  That she forget us not in after years;
    For we have seen the light, and it
      were grievous
    To dim that dawning if our lady leave
    us.

By life that ebbed with none to stanch the
    failing,
By Love's sad harvest garnered in the spring,
When Love in ignorance wept unavailing
  O'er young buds dead before their blos-
    soming;
    By all the gray owl watched, the pale
      moon viewed,
    In past grim years, declare our grati-
      tude!

By hands uplifted to the Gods that heard
    not,
By gifts that found no favor in their sight,

By faces bent above the babe that stirred
    not,
  By nameless horrors of the stifling night;
    By ills foredone, by peace her toils
      discover,
    Bid Earth be good beneath and
    Heaven above her!

If she have sent her servants in our pain,
  If she have fought with Death and dulled
    his sword;
If she have given back our sick again,
  And to the breast the weakling lips
    restored,
    Is it a little thing that she has wrought?
    Then Life and Death and Motherhood
    be nought.

Go forth, O wind, our message on thy wings,
  And they shall hear thee pass and bid thee
    speed,
In reed-roofed hut, or white-walled home of
  kings,
  Who have been helpen by her in their
  need.

All spring shall give thee fragrance,
   and the wheat
Shall be a tasselled floorcloth to thy
   feet.

Haste, for our hearts are with thee, take no
   rest !
Loud-voiced ambassador, from sea to sea
Proclaim the blessing, manifold, confest,
   Of those in darkness by her hand set free,
     Then very softly to her presence move,
     And whisper: " Lady, lo, they know
      and love !"

Ballad of Fisher's Boarding-House.

THAT night, when through the mooring-chains
  The wide-eyed corpse rolled free,
To blunder down by Garden Reach
  And rot at Kedgeree,
The tale the Hughli told the shoal
  The lean shoal told to me.

'TWAS Fultah Fisher's boarding-house
  Where sailor-men reside,
And there were men of all the ports
  From Mississip to Clyde,
And regally they spat and smoked,
  And fearsomely they lied.

They lied about the purple Sea
  That gave them scanty bread,
They lied about the Earth beneath,
  The Heavens overhead,
For they had looked too often on
  Black rum when that was red.

They told their tales of wreck and wrong,
  Of shame and lust and fraud,
They backed their toughest statements with
  The Brimstone of the Lord,
And crackling oaths went to and fro
  Across the fist-banged board.

And there was Hans the blue-eyed Dane,
   Bull-throated, bare of arm,
Who carried on his hairy chest
   The maid Ultruda's charm—
The little silver crucifix
   That keeps a man from harm.

And there was Jake Without-the-Ears,
   And Pamba the Malay,
And Carboy Gin the Guinea cook,
   And Luz from Vigo Bay,
And Honest Jack who sold them slops
   And harvested their pay.

And there was Salem Hardieker,
   A lean Bostonian he—
Russ, German, English, Halfbreed, Finn,
   Yank, Dane, and Portugee,
At Fultah Fisher's boarding-house
   They rested from the sea.

Now Anne of Austria shared their drinks,
   Collinga knew her fame,
From Tarnau in Galicia
   To Jaun Bazar she came,
To eat the bread of infamy
   And take the wage of shame.

She held a dozen men to heel—
    Rich spoil of war was hers,
In hose and gown and ring and chain,
    From twenty mariners,
And, by Port Law, that week, men called
    Her Salem Hardieker's.

But seamen learnt—what landsmen know-
    That neither gifts nor gain
Can hold a winking Light o' Love
    Or Fancy's flight restrain,
When Anne of Austria rolled her eyes
    On Hans the blue-eyed Dane.

Since Life is strife, and strife means knife,
    From Howrah to the Bay,
And he may die before the dawn
    Who liquored out the day,
In Fultah Fisher's boarding-house
    We woo while yet we may.

But cold was Hans the blue-eyed Dane,
    Bull-throated, bare of arm,
And laughter shook the chest beneath
    The maid Ultruda's charm—
The little silver crucifix
    That keeps a man from harm.

"You speak to Salem Hardieker,
　You was his girl, I know.
I ship mineselfs to-morrow, see,
　Und round the Skaw we go,
South, down the Cattegat, by Hjelm,
　To Besser in Saro."

When love rejected turns to hate,
　All ill betide the man.
"You speak to Salem Hardieker"—
　She spoke as woman can.
A scream—a sob—"He called me—names!"
　And then the fray began.

An oath from Salem Hardieker,
　A shriek upon the stairs,
A dance of shadows on the wall,
　A knife-thrust unawares—
And Hans came down, as cattle drop,
　Across the broken chairs.

　　　·　　　·　　　·　　　·　　　·

In Anne of Austria's trembling hands
　The weary head fell low:—
"I ship mineselfs to-morrow, straight
　For Besser in Saro:
Und there Ultruda comes to me
　At Easter, und I go

"South, down the Cattegat—   What's here?
  There—are—no—lights—to—guide!"
The mutter ceased, the spirit passed,
  And Anne of Austria cried
In Fultah Fisher's boarding-house
  When Hans the mighty died.

Thus slew they Hans the blue-eyed Dane,
  Bull-throated, bare of arm,
But Anne of Austria looted first
  The maid Ultruda's charm—
The little silver crucifix
  That keeps a man from harm.

"As the Bell Clinks."

AS I left the Halls at Lumley, rose the
    vision of a comely
Maid last season worshipped dumbly,
    watched with fervor from afar;
And I wondered idly, blindly, if the maid
    would greet me kindly.
That was all—the rest was settled by the
    clinking tonga-bar.
Yea, my life and hers were coupled by the
    tonga coupling-bar.

For my misty meditation, at the second
    changing-station,
Suffered sudden dislocation, fled before the
    tuneless jar
Of a Wagner *obbligato*, *scherzo*, double-hand
    staccato,
Played on either pony's saddle by the clack-
    ing tonga-bar—
Played with human speech, I fancied, by
    the jigging, jolting bar.

"She was sweet," thought I, "last season,
  but 'twere surely wild unreason
Such tiny hope to freeze on as was offered
  by my Star,
When she whispered, something sadly:—'I
  —we feel your going badly!'"
"*And you let the chance escape you?*" rapped
  the rattling tonga-bar.
"*What a chance and what an idiot!*" clicked
  the vicious tonga-bar.

Heart of man—oh, heart of putty! Had I
  gone by Kakahutti,
On the old Hill-road and rutty, I had 'scaped
  that fatal car,
But his fortune each must bide by, so I
  watched the milestones slide by,
To "*You call on Her to-morrow!*"—fugue with
  cymbals by the bar—
"*You must call on Her to-morrow!*"—post-
  horn gallop by the bar.

Yet a further stage my goal on—we were
  whirling down to Solon,
With a double lurch and roll on, best foot
  foremost, *ganz und gar*—

"She was *very* sweet," I hinted. "If a kiss
 had been imprinted—?"
" '*Would ha' saved a world of trouble !*" clashed
 the busy tonga-bar.
" '*Been accepted or rejected !*" banged and
 clanged the tonga-bar.

Then a notion wild and daring, 'spite the
 income tax's paring,
And a hasty thought of sharing—less than
 many incomes are,
Made me put a question private, you can
 guess what I would drive at.
" *You must work the sum to prove it* " clanked
 the careless tonga-bar.
" *Simple Rule of Two will prove it* " lilted back
 the tonga-bar.

It was under Khyraghaut I mused :—"Sup-
 pose the maid be haughty—
(There are lovers rich—and forty)—wait
 some wealthy Avatar?
Answer, monitor untiring, 'twixt the ponies
 twain perspiring !"
" *Faint heart never won fair lady* " creaked the
 straining tonga-bar.
" *Can I tell you ere you ask Her ?*" pounded
 slow the tonga-bar.

Last, the Tara Devi turning showed the
   lights of Simla burning,
Lit my little lazy yearning to a fiercer
   flame by far.
As below the Mall we jingled, through my
   very heart it tingled—
Did the iterated order of the threshing tonga-
   bar—
"*Try your luck—you can't do better!*" twanged
   the loosened tonga-bar.

An Old Song.

SO long as 'neath the Kalka hills,
   The tonga-horn shall ring,
So long as down the Solon dip
   The hard-held ponies swing,
So long as Tara Devi sees
   The lights o' Simla town,
So long as Pleasure calls us up,
   And duty drives us down,
     If you love me as I love you,
     What pair so happy as we two?

So long as Aces take the King,
   Or backers take the bet,
So long as debt leads men to wed,
   Or marriage leads to debt,
So long as little luncheons, Love,
   And scandal hold their vogue,
While there is sport at Annandale
   Or whiskey at Jutogh,
     If you love me as I love you,
     What knife can cut our love in two?

(137)

So long as down the rocking floor
    The raving polka spins,
So long as Kitchen Lancers spur
    The maddened violins,
So long as through the whirling smoke
    We hear the oft-told tale :—
" Twelve hundred in the Lotteries,"
    And *Whatshername* for sale?
      If you love me as I love you,
      We'll play the game and win it too.

So long as Lust or Lucre tempt
    Straight riders from the course,
So long as with each drink we pour
    Black brewage of Remorse,
So long as those unloaded guns
    We keep beside the bed
Blow off, by obvious accident,
    The lucky owner's head,
      If you love me as I love you,
      What can Life kill or Death undo?

So long as Death 'twixt dance and dance
    Chills best and bravest blood,
And drops the reckless rider down
    The rotten, rain-soaked *khud,*

So long as rumors from the North
　Make loving wives afraid,
So long as Burma takes the boy
　And typhoid kills the maid,
　　If you love me as I love you,
　　What knife can cut our love in two?

By all that lights our daily life
　Or works our lifelong woe,
From Boileaugunge to Simla Downs
　And those grim glades below,
Where, heedless of the flying hoof
　And clamor overhead,
Sleep, with the gray langur for guard,
　Our very scornful Dead,
　　If you love me as I love you,
　　All Earth is servant to us two?

By Docket, Billetuoux, and File,
　By Mountain, Cliff, and Fir,
By Fan and Sword and Office-box,
　By Corset, Plume, and Spur,
By Riot, Revel, Waltz, and War,
　By Women, Work, and Bills,
By all the life that fizzes in
　The everlasting Hills,
　　If you love me as I love you,
　　What pair so happy as we two?

Certain Maxims of Hafiz.

I.

IF It be pleasant to look on, stalled in the
packed *serai*,
Does not the Young Man try Its temper and
pace ere he buy?
If She be pleasant to look on, what does the
Young Man say?
" Lo! She is pleasant to look on, give Her
to me to-day!"

II.

Yea, though a Kafir die, to him is remitted
Jehannum
If he borrowed in life from a native at sixty
per cent. per annum.

III.

Blister we not for *bursati?* So when the heart
is vext,
The pain of one maiden's refusal is drowned
in the pain of the next.

IV.

The temper of chums, the love of your wife,
  and a new piano's tune—
Which of the three will you trust at the end
  of an Indian June?

V.

Who are the rulers of Ind—to whom shall
  we bow the knee?
Make your peace with the women, and men
  will make you L. G.

VI.

Does the woodpecker flit round the young
  ferash? Does grass clothe a new-built
  wall?
Is she under thirty, the woman who holds a
  boy in her thrall?

VII.

If She grow suddenly gracious—reflecc. Is
  it all for thee?
The black-buck is stalked through the bul-
  lock, and Man through jealousy.

VIII.

Seek not for favor of women.   So shall you
find it indeed.
Does not the boar break cover just when
you're lighting a weed?

IX.

If He play, being young and unskilful, for
shekels of silver and gold,
Take His money, my son, praising Allah,
The kid was ordained to be sold.

X.

With a " weed " among men or horses verily
this is the best,
That you work him in office or dog-cart
lightly—but give him no rest.

XI.

Pleasant the snaffle of Courtship, improving
the manners and carriage;
But the colt who is wise will abstain from
the terrible thorn-bit of Marriage.

XII.

As the thriftless gold of the *babul*, so is the
gold that we spend
On a Derby Sweep, or our neighbor's wife.
or the horse that we buy from a friend.

XIII.

The ways of man with a maid be strange,
yet simple and tame
To the ways of a man with a horse, when
selling or racing that same.

XIV.

In public Her face turneth to thee, and
pleasant Her smile when ye meet.
It is ill. The cold rocks of El-Gidar smile
thus on the waves at their feet.
In public Her face is averted, with anger
She nameth thy name.
It is well. Was there ever a loser content
with the loss of the game?

XV.

If She have spoken a word, remember thy
lips are sealed,
And the Brand of the Dog is upon him by
whom is the secret revealed.

If She have written a letter, delay not an instant, but burn it.

Tear it in pieces, O Fool. and the wind to her mate shall return it!

If there be trouble to Herward, and a lie of the blackest can clear,

Lie, while thy lips can move or a man is alive to hear.

XVI.

My Son, if a maiden deny thee and scufflingly bid thee give o'er,

Yet lip meets with lip at the lastward—get out! She has been there before.

They are pecked on the ear and the chin and the nose who are lacking in lore.

XVII.

If we fall in the race, though we win, the hoof-slide is scarred on the course.

Though Allah and Earth pardon Sin, remaineth forever Remorse.

XVIII.

" By all I am misunderstood!" if the Matron shall say, or the Maid :—

" Alas! I do not understand," my son, be thou nowise afraid.

In vain in the sight of the Bird is the net
of the fowler displayed.

XIX.

My son, if I, Hafiz, thy father, take hold of
thy knees in my pain,
Demanding thy name on stamped paper,
one day, or one hour—refrain.
Are the links of thy fetters so light that thou
cravest another man's chain?

The Grave of the Hundred Head.

THERE'S a widow in sleepy Chester
  Who weeps for her only son ;
There's a grave on the Pabeng River,
  A grave that the Burmans shun,
And there's Subadar Prag Tewarri
  Who tells how the work was done.

A Snider squibbed in the jungle,·
  Somebody laughed and fled,
And the men of the First Shikaris
  Picked up their Subaltern dead,
With a big blue mark in his forehead
  And the back blown out of his head.

Subadar Prag Tewarri,
  Jemadar Hira Lal,
Took command of the party,
  Twenty rifles in all,
Marched them down to the river
  As the day was beginning to fall.
  (146)

They buried the boy by the river,
   A blanket over his face—
They wept for their dead Lieutenant,
   The men of an alien race—
They made a *samádh* in his honor,
   A mark for his resting-place.

For they swore by the Holy Water,
   They swore by the salt they ate,
That the soul of Lieutenant Eshmitt Sahib
   Should go to his God in state ;
With fifty file of Burman
   To open him Heaven's gate.

The men of the First Shikaris
   Marched till the break of day,
Till they came to the rebel village,
   The village of Pabengmay—
A *jingal* covered the clearing,
   Calthrops hampered the way

Subadar Prag Tewarri,
   Bidding them load with ball,
Halted a dozen rifles
   Under the village wall;
Sent out a flanking-party
   With Jemadar Hira Lal.

The men of the First Shikaris
  Shouted and smote and slew,
Turning the grinning *jingal*
  On to the howling crew.
The Jemadar's flanking-party
  Butchered the folk who flew.

Long was the morn of slaughter,
  Long was the list of slain,
Five score heads were taken,
  Five score heads and twain;
And the men of the First Shikaris
  Went back to their grave again,

Each man bearing a basket
  Red as his palms that day,
Red as the blazing village—
  The village of Pabengmay.
And the " *drip-drip-drip* " from the baskets
  Reddened the grass by the way.

They made a pile of their trophies
  High as a tall man's chin,
Head upon head distorted,
  Set in a sightless grin,
Anger and pain and terror
  Stamped on the smoke-scorched skin.

Subadar Prag Tewarri
  Put the head of the Boh
On the top of the mound of triumph,
  The head of his son below,
With the sword and the peacock-banner
  That the world might behold and know.

Thus the *samádh* was perfect,
  Thus was the lesson plain
Of the wrath of the First Shikaris—
  The price of a white man slain;
And the men of the First Shikaris
  Went back into camp again.

Then a silence came to the river,
  A hush fell over the shore,
And Bohs that were brave departed,
  And Sniders squibbed no more;
    For the Burmans said,
    That a *kullah's* head
Must be paid for with heads five score.

There's a widow in sleepy Chester
  Who weeps for her only son;
There's a grave on the Pabeng River,
  A grave that the Burmans shun,
And there's Subadar Prag Tewarri
  Who tells how the work was done.

The Overland Mail.

(Foot-Service to the Hills.)

IN the name of the Empress of India, make
  way,
    O Lords of the Jungle, wherever you
    roam.
The woods are astir at the close of the day—
    We exiles are waiting for letters from
    Home.
Let the robber retreat—let the tiger turn
  tail—
In the Name of the Empress, the Overland
  Mail!

With a jingle of bells as the dusk gathers in,
    He turns to the foot-path that heads up
    hill—
The bags on his back and a cloth round his
  chin,
    And, tucked in his waist-belt, the Post
    Office bill:—
"Despatched on this date, as received by
  the rail,
Per runner, two bags of the Overland Mail."

Is the torrent in spate? He must ford it or
  swim.
  Has the rain wrecked the road? He
  must climb by the cliff.
Does the tempest cry "Halt"? What are
  tempests to him?
  The Service admits not a "but" or an
  "if."
While the breath's in his mouth, he must
  bear without fail,
In the name of the Empress, the Overland
  Mail.

From aloe to rose-oak, from rose-oak to fir,
  From level to upland, from upland to
  crest,
From rice-field to rock-ridge, from rock-
  ridge to spur,
  Fly the soft sandalled feet, strains the
  brawny brown chest.
From rail to ravine—to the peak from the
  vale—
Up, up through the night goes the Overland
  Mail.

There's a speck on the hillside, a dot on the
  road—

A jingle of bells on the foot-path below—
There's a scuffle above in the monkey's
    abode—
  The world is awake, and the clouds are
    aglow.
For the great Sun himself must attend to the
    hail :—
" In the name of the Empress, the Overland
    Mail !"

What the People Said.

(*June* 21, 1887.)

BY the well, where the bullocks go
Silent and blind and slow—
By the field where the young corn dies
In the face of the sultry skies,
They have heard, as the dull earth hears
The voice of the wind of an hour,
The sound of the Great Queen's voice:—
"My God hath given me years,
Hath granted dominion and power:
And I bid you, O Land, rejoice."

And the ploughman settles the share
More deep in the grudging clod;
For he saith: "The wheat is my care,
And the rest is the will of God.
He sent the Mahratta spear
As He sendeth the rain,
And the *Mlech*, in the fated year,
Broke the spear in twain,

And was broken in turn.   Who knows
How our Lords make strife?
It is good that the young wheat grows,
For the bread is Life."

Then, far and near, as the twilight drew,
   Hissed up to the scornful dark
Great serpents, blazing, of red and blue,
That rose and faded, and rose anew,
   That the Land might wonder and mark.
" To-day is a day of days," they said,
" Make merry, O People, all!"
And the Ploughman listened and bowed his
     head :—
" To-day and to-morrow God's will," he said,
As he trimmed the lamps on the wall.

" He sendeth us years that are good,
As He sendeth the dearth.
He giveth to each man his food,
Or Her food to the Earth.
Our Kings and our Queens are afar—
On their peoples be peace—
God bringeth the rain to the Bar,
That our cattle increase."

And the Ploughman settled the share
More deep in the sun-dried clod :—

" Mogul, Mahratta, and *Mlech* from the North,
And White Queen over the Seas—
God raiseth them up and driveth them forth
As the dust of the ploughshare flies in the
    breeze ;
But the wheat and the cattle are all my care
And the rest is the will of God."

The Undertaker's Horse.

"To-tschin-shu is condemned to death. How can he drink tea with the Executioner?"—*Japanese Proverb.*

THE eldest son bestrides him
And the pretty daughter rides him,
And I meet him oft o' mornings on the
  Course;
And there wakens in my bosom
An emotion chill and gruesome
As I canter past the Undertaker's Horse.

Neither shies ne nor is restive,
But a hideously suggestive
Trot, professional and placid, he affects;
And the cadence of his hoof-beats
To my mind, this grim reproof beats:—
"Mend your pace, my friend, I'm coming.
  Who's the next?"

Ah! stud-bred of ill-omen,
I have watched the strongest go—men
Of pith and might and muscle—at your
  heels,

(156)

Down the plantain-bordered highway,
(Heaven send it ne'er be my way!)
In a lacquered box and jetty upon wheels.

Answer, sombre beast and dreary,
Where is Brown, the young, the cheery,
Smith, the pride of all his friends and half
   the Force?
You were at that last dread *dak*
We must cover at a walk,
Bring them back to me, O Undertaker's
   Horse!

With your mane unhogged and flowing,
And your curious way of going,
And that business-like black crimping of.
   your tail,
E'en with Beauty on your back, sir,
Pacing as a lady's hack, sir,
What wonder when I meet you I turn pale?

It may be you wait your time, Beast,
Till I write my last bad rhyme, Beast,
Quit the sunlight, cut the rhyming, drop
   the glass,
Follow after with the others,
Where some dusky heathen smothers
Us with marigolds in lieu of English grass.

Or, perchance, in years to follow,
I shall watch your plump sides hollow,
See Carnifex (gone lame) become a corse,
See old age at last o'erpower you,
And the Station Pack devour you,
I shall chuckle then, O Undertaker's Horse!

But to insult, gibe, and quest, I've
Still the hideously suggestive
Trot that hammers out the grim and warn-
　　ing text,
And I hear it hard behind me,
In what place soe'er I find me :—
"Sure to catch you sooner or later.　Who's
　　the next?"

Arithmetic on the Frontier.

A GREAT and glorious thing it is
   To learn, for seven years or so,
The Lord knows what of that and this,
   Ere reckoned fit to face the foe—
The flying bullet down the Pass,
That whistles clear: "All flesh is grass."

Three hundred pounds per annum spent
   On making brain and body meeter
For all the murderous intent
   Comprised in "villanous saltpetre!"
And after—ask the Yusuzaies
What comes of all our 'ologies.

A scrimmage in a Border Station—
   A canter down some dark defile—
Two thousand pounds of education
   Drops to a ten-rupee *jezail*—
The Crammer's boast, the Squadron's pride,
Shot like a rabbit in a ride!

No proposition Euclid wrote,
  No formulæ the text-books know,
Will turn the bullet from your coat,
  Or ward the tulwar's downward blow.
Strike hard who cares—shoot straight who
    can—
The odds are on the cheaper man.

One sword-knot stolen from the camp
  Will pay for all the school expenses
Of any Kurrum Valley scamp
  Who knows no word or moods and tenses,
But, being blessed with perfect sight,
Picks off our messmates left and right.

With home-bred hordes the hill-sides teem,
  The troop-ships bring us one by one,
At vast expense of time and steam,
  To slay Alfridis where they run.
The " captives of our bow and spear "
Are cheap—alas ! as we are dear.

One Viceroy Resigns.

(Lord Dufferin to Lord Lansdowne.)

SO here's your Empire. No more wine,.
then ? Good.

We'll clear the Aides and *khitmatgars* away.

(You'll know that fat old fellow with the·
knife—

He keeps the Name Book, talks in English
too,

And almost thinks himself the Govern-
ment.)

O Youth, Youth, Youth ! Forgive me, you're·
so young.

Forty from sixty—twenty years of work

And power to back the working. *Ay de mi !*

You want to know, you want to see, to touch,

And, by your lights, to act. It's natural.

I wonder can I help you. Let me try.

You saw—what did you see from Bombay
east?

Enough to frighten any one but me?

Neat that ! It frightened Me in Eighty-
Four!

You shouldn't take a man from Canada

And bid him smoke in powder-magazines ;
Nor with a Reputation such as—Bah !
That ghost has haunted me for twenty years.
My Reputation now full blown—Your
    fault—
Yours, with your stories of the strife at
    Home,
Who's up, who's down, who leads and who
    is led—
One reads so much, one hears so little here.
Well, now's your turn of exile. I go back
To Rome and leisure. All roads lead to
    Rome,
Or books—the refuge of the destitute.
When you . . . that brings me back to In-
    dia. See !
    Start clear. I couldn't. Egypt served
      my turn.
You'll never plumb the Oriental mind,
And if you did it isn't worth the toil.
Think of a sleek French priest in Canada ;
Divide by twenty half-breeds. Multiply
By twice the Sphinx's silence. There's
    your East,
And you're as wise as ever. So am I.
    Accept on trust and work in darkness,
      strike

At venture, stumble forward, make your
  mark,
(It's chalk on granite), then thank God no
  flame
Leaps from the rock to shrivel mark and
  man.
I'm clear—my mark is made. Three months
  of drought
Had ruined much. It rained and washed
  away
The specks that might have gathered on my
  Name.
I took a country twice the size of France,
And shuttered up one doorway in the North.
I stand by those. You'll find that both will
  pay,
I pledged my Name on both—they're yours
  to-night.
Hold to them—they hold fame enough for
  two.
I'm old, but I shall live till Burma pays.
Men there—*not* German traders—Cr–sthw–te
  knows—
You'll find it in my papers. For the North
Guns always—quietly—but always guns.
You've seen your Council? Yes, they'll **try**
  to rule,

And prize their Reputations.   Have you met
A grim lay-reader with a taste for coins,
And faith in Sin most men withhold from
  God?
He's gone to England.   R–p–n knew his
  grip
And kicked.   A Council always has its
  H–pes.
˙They look for nothing from the West but
  Death
·Or Bath or Bournemouth.   Here's their
  ground.
                                    They fight
·Until the middle classes take them back,
One of ten millions plus a C. S. I.
Or drop in harness.   Legion of the Lost?
Not altogether—earnest, narrow men,
But chiefly earnest, and they'll do your work,
And end by writing letters to the *Times.*
(Shall *I* write letters, answering H–nt–r—
  fawn
With R–p–n on the Yorkshire grocers?
  Ugh!)
They have their Reputations.   Look to one—
I work with him—the smallest of them all,
White-haired, red-faced, who sat the plung-
  ing horse

Out in the garden. He's your right-hand
    man,
And dreams of tilting W–ls–y from the
    throne,
But while he dreams gives work we cannot
    buy ;
He has his Reputation—wants the Lords
By way of Frontier Roads. Meantime, I
    think,
He values very much the hand that falls
Upon his shoulder at the Council table—
Hates cats and knows his business: *which is*
    yours.
    Your business ! Twice a hundred mil-
      lion souls.
Your business ! I could tell you what I
    did
Some nights of Eighty-Five, at Simla, worth
A Kingdom's ransom. When a big ship
    drives,
God knows to what new reef the man at the
    wheel
Prays with the passengers. They lose their
    lives,
Or rescued go their way ; but he's no man
To take his trick at the wheel again—that's
    ʾ ɔrse

Than drowning. Well, a galled Mashobra
    mule
(You'll see Mashobra) passed me on the
    Mall,
And I was—some fool's wife had ducked
    and bowed
To show the others I would stop and speak.
Then the mule fell—three galls, a hand-
    breadth each,
Behind the withers. Mrs. Whatsisname
Leers at the mule and me by turns, thweet
    thoul!
"How could they make him carry such a
    load!"
I saw—it isn't often I dream dreams—
More than the mule that minute—smoke
    and flame
From Simla to the haze below. That's
    weak.
You're younger. You'll dream dreams be-
    fore you've done.
You've youth, that's one—good workmen—
    that means two
Fair chances in your favor. Fate's the third.
I know what *I* did. Do you ask me,
    " Preach?"
I answer by my past or else go back

To platitudes of rule—or take you thus
In confidence and say :—" You know the
    trick :
You've governed Canada. You know. *You*
    know!"
And all the while commend you to Fate's
    hand
(Here at the top one loses sight o' God),
Commend you, then, to something more
    than you—
The Other People's blunders and . . .
    that's all.
I'd agonize to serve you if I could.
It's incommunicable, like the cast
That drops the tackle with the gut adry.
Too much—too little—there's your salmon
    lost!
And so I tell you nothing—wish you luck,
And wonder—how I wonder!—for your
    sake
And triumph for my own. You're young,
    you're young,
You hold to half a hundred Shibboleths.
I'm old. I followed Power to the last,
Gave her my best, and Power followed Me.
It's worth it—on my soul I'm speaking
    plain,

Here by the claret glasses!—worth it all.

I gave—no matter what I gave—I win.

I *know* I win. Mine's work, good work that
live!

A country twice the size of France—the
North

Safeguarded. That's my record: sink the
rest

And better if you can. The Rains may
serve,

Rupees may rise—three pence will give you
Fame—

It's rash to hope for sixpence—If they rise

Get guns, more guns, and lift the salt-tax.
                                    Oh!

I told you what the Congress meant or
thought?

I'll answer nothing. Half a year will prove

The full extent of time and thought you'll
spare.

To Congress. Ask a Lady Doctor *once*

How little Begums see the light—deduce

Thence how the True Reformer's child v
born.

It's interesting, curious . . . and vile.

I told the Turk he was a gentleman.

I told the Russian that his Tartar veins

Bled pure Parisian ichor ; and he purred.

The Congress doesn't purr. I think it swears.

You're young—you'll swear too ere you've
    reached the end.

The End ! God help you, if there be a God.

(There must be one to startle Gl–dst–ne's
    soul

In that new land where all the wires are cut,

And Cr–ss snores anthems on the asphodel).

God help you ! And I'd help you if I could.

But that's beyond me. Yes, your speech
    was crude.

Sound claret after olives—yours and mine ;

But Medoc slips into vin ordinaire.

(I'll drink my first at Genoa to your health.)

Raise it to Hock. You'll never catch my
    style.

And, after all, the middle-classes grip

The middle-class—for Brompton talk Earl's
    Court.

Perhaps you're right. I'll see you in the
    Times—

A quarter-column of eye-searing print,

A leader once a quarter—then a war ;

The Strand abellow through the fog : " De-
    feat !"

"'Orrible slaughter !" While you lie awake

And wonder.   Oh, you'll wonder ere you're
   free !
I wonder now.   The four years slide away
So fast, so fast, and leave me here alone.
R—y, C–lv–n, L—l, R–b–rts, B–ck, the rest,
Princes and Powers of Darkness, troops and
   trains,
(I *cannot* sleep in trains), land piled on land,
Whitewash and weariness, red rockets, dust,
White snows that mocked me, palaces—with
   draughts,
And W–stl–nd with the drafts he couldn't
   pay,
Poor W–ls–n reading his obituary
Before he died, and H–pe, the man with
   bones,
And A–tch–s–n a dripping mackintosh
At Council in the Rains, his grating "Sirrr"
Half drowned by H–nt–r's silky :—" Bat my
   lahd."
Hunterian always : M–rsh–l spinning plates
Or standing on his head ; the Rent Bill's
   roar,
A hundred thousand speeches, much red
   cloth,
And Smiths thrice happy if I call them
   Jones,

(I can't remember half their names) or
    reined
My pony on the Mall to greet their wives.
More trains, more troops, more dust, and
    then all's done.
Four years, and I forget.　If I forget
How will *they* bear me in their minds?　The
    North
Safeguarded—nearly　(R–b–rts knows the
    rest),
A country twice the size of France annexed.
That stays at least.　The rest may pass—
    may pass—
Your heritage—and I can teach you nought.
" High trust," " vast honor," " interests twice
    as vast,"
" Due reverence to your Council "—keep to
    those.
I envy you the twenty years you've gained,
But not the five to follow.　What's that?
    One?
Two!—Surely not so late.　Good-night.
    Don't dream.

The Betrothed

"You must choose between me and your cigar."

OPEN the old cigar-box, get me a Cuba
    stout,.
For things are running crossways, and
    Maggie and I are out.

We quarrelled about Havanas—we fought
    o'er a good cheroot,
And I know she is exacting, and she says I
    am a brute.

Open the old cigar-box—let me consider a
    space;
In the soft blue veil of the vapor, musing on
    Maggie's face.

Maggie is pretty to look at—Maggie's a loving
    lass,
But the prettiest cheeks must wrinkle, the
    truest of loves must pass.

(172)

There's peace in a Laranaga, there's calm in
  a Henry Clay,
But the best cigar in an hour is finished and
  thrown away—

Thrown away for another as perfect and ripe
  and brown—
But I could not throw away Maggie for fear
  o' the talk o' the town !

Maggie, my wife at fifty—gray and dour and
  old—
With never another Maggie to purchase for
  love or gold !

And the light of Days that have Been, the
  dark of the Days that Are,
And Love's torch stinking and stale, like the
  butt of a dead cigar—

The butt of a dead cigar you are bound to
  keep in your pocket—
With never a new one to light tho' it's charred
  and black to the socket.

Open the old cigar-box—let me consider a
  while—
Here is a mild Manilla—there is a wifely
  smile.

Which is the better portion—bondage bought
  with a ring,
Or a harem of dusky beauties fifty tied in a
  string?

Counsellors cunning and silent—comforters
  true and tried,
And never a one of the fifty to sneer at a
  rival bride.

Thought in the early morning, solace in time
  of woes,
Peace in the hush of the twilight, balm ere
  my eyelids close.

This will the fifty give me, asking nought in
  return,
With only a *Suttee's* passion—to do their
  duty and burn. ·

This will the fifty give me. When they are
  spent and dead,
Five times other fifties shall be my servants
  instead.

The furrows of far-off Java, the isles of the
  Spanish Main,
When they hear my harem is empty, will
  send me my brides again.

I will take no heed to their raiment, nor
food for their mouths withal,
So long as the gulls are nesting, so long as
the showers fall.

I will scent 'em with best vanilla, with tea
will I temper their hides,
And the Moor and the Mormon shall envy
who read of the tale of my brides.

For Maggie has written a letter to give me
my choice between
The wee little whimpering Love and the
great god Nick o' Teen.   . .

And I have been servant of Love for barely
a twelvemonth clear,
But I have been Priest of Partagas a matter
of seven year ;

And the gloom of my bachelor days is
necked with the cheery light
Of stumps that I burned to Friendship and
Pleasure and Work and Fight.

And I turn my eyes to the future that Maggie
and I must prove,
But the only light on the marshes is the
Will-o'-the-Wisp of Love.

Will it see me safe through my journey, or
    leave me bogged in the mire?
Since a puff of tobacco can cloud it, shall I
    follow the fitful fire?

Open the old cigar-box—let me consider
    anew—
Old friends, and who is Maggie that I should
    abandon *you?*

A million surplus Maggies are willing to
    bear the yoke;
And a woman is only a woman, but a good
    cigar is a Smoke.

Light me another Cuba; I hold to my first-
    sworn vows,
If Maggie will have no rival, I'll have no
    Maggie for spouse!

A Tale of Two Cities.

WHERE the sober-colored cultivator smiles
      On his *byles;*
Where the cholera, the cyclone, and the
   crow
      Come and go;
Where the merchant deals in indigo and tea,
      Hides and *ghi;*
Where the Babu drops inflammatory hints
      In his prints;
Stands a City—Charnock chose it—packed
   away
      Near a Bay—
By the sewage rendered fetid, by the sewer
      Made impure,
By the Sunderbunds unwholesome, by the
   swamp
      Moist and damp;
And the City and the Viceroy, as we see,
      Don't agree.
Once, two hundred years ago, the trader
   came
      Meek and tame.

12   (177)

Where his timid foot first halted, there he
    stayed,
        Till mere trade
Grew to Empire, and he sent his armies
    forth
        South and North
Till the country from Peshawar to Ceylon
        Was his own.
Thus the mid-day halt of Charnock—more's
    the pity!
        Grew a City.
As the fungus sprouts chaotic from its bed,
        So it spread—
Chance-directed, chance-erected, laid and
    built
        On the silt—
Palace, byre, hovel—poverty and pride—
        Side by side;
And, above the packed and pestilential town,
        Death looked down.
But the Rulers in that City by the Sea
        Turned to flee—
Fled, with each returning spring-tide from
    its ills
        To the Hills.
From the clammy fogs of morning, from the
    blaze
        Of the days,

From the sickness of the noontide, from the
 heat,
    Beat retreat;
For the country from Peshawar to Ceylon
    Was their own.
But the Merchant risked the perils of the
 Plain
    For his gain.
Now the resting-place of Charnock, 'neath
 the palms,
    Asks an alms,
And the burden of its lamentation is,
    Briefly, this :
" Because, for certain months, we boil and
 stew,
    So should you.
Cast the Viceroy and his Council to perspire
    In our fire !"
And for answer to the argument, in vain
    We explain
That an amateur Saint Lawrence cannot
 fry :—
    " *All* must fry !"
That the Merchant risks the perils of the
 Plain
    For his gain,
Nor can Rulers rule a house that men grow
 rich in,
    From its kitchen.

Let the Babu drop inflammatory hints
　　　　In his prints;
And mature—consistent soul—his plan for
　　stealing
　　　　To Darjeeling:
Let the Merchant seek, who makes his silver
　　pile,
　　　　England's isle;
Let the City Charnock pitched on—evil
　　day!—
　　　　Go Her way.
Though the argosies of Asia at Her doors
　　　　Heap their stores,
Though Her enterprise and energy secure
　　　　Income sure,
Though "out-station orders punctually
　　obeyed"
　　　　Swell her trade—
Still, for rule, administration, and the rest,
　　　　Simla's best.

Griffen's Debt.

IMPRIMIS he was "broke."   Thereafter left
His regiment, and, later, took to drink ;
Then, having lost the balance of his friends,
"Went Fantee"—joined the people of the land,
Turned three parts Mussulman and one Hindu,
And lived among the Gauri villagers,
Who gave him shelter and a wife or twain,
And boasted that a thorough, full-blood *sahib*
Had come among them.   Thus he spent his time,
Deeply indebted to the village *shroff*,
(Who never asked for payment) always drunk,
Unclean, abominable, out-at-heels ;
Forgetting that he was an Englishman.

You know they dammed the Gauri with a dam,
And all the good contractors scamped their work,

And all the bad material at hand
Was used to dam the Gauri—which was
  cheap,
And, therefore proper. Then the Gauri
  burst,
And several hundred thousand cubic tons
Of water dropped into the valley, *flop*,
And drowned some five and twenty vil-
  lagers,
And did a lakh or two of detriment
To crops and cattle. When the flood went
  down
We found him dead, beneath an old dead
  horse,
Full six miles down the valley. So we said
He was a victim to the Demon Drink,
And moralized upon him for a week,
And then forgot him. Which was natural.

But, in the valley of the Gauri, men
Beneath the shadow of the big new dam
Relate a foolish legend of the flood,
Accounting for the little loss of life
(Only those five and twenty villagers)
In this wise: On the evening of the flood,
They heard the groaning of the rotten dam,
And voices of the Mountain Devils. Then

An incarnation of the local God,
Mounted upon a monster-neighing horse,
And flourishing a flail-like whip, came down,
Breathing ambrosia, to the villages,
And fell upon the simple villagers
With yells beyond the power of mortal
throat,
And blows beyond the power of mortal
hand,
And smote them with the flail-like whip, and
drove
Them clamorous with terror up the hill,
And scattered, with the monster-neighing
steed,
Their crazy cottages about their ears,
And generally cleared those villages.
Then came the water, and the local God,
Breathing ambrosia, flourishing his whip,
And mounted on his monster-neighing
steed,
Went down the valley with the flying trees
And residue of homesteads, while they
watched
Safe on the mountain-side these wondrous
things,
And knew that they were much beloved of
Heaven.

Wherefore, and when the dam was newly
  built,
They raised a temple to the local God,
And burned all manner of unsavory things
Upon his altar and created priests,
And blew into a conch, and banged a bell,
And told the story of the Gauri flood
With circumstance and much embroidery.

So he the whiskified Objectionable,
Unclean, abominable, out-at-heels,
Became the tutelary Deity
Of all the Gauri valley villages;
And may in time become a Solar Myth.

The Galley-Slave.

OH, gallant was our galley from her carven
    steering-wheel
To her figurehead of silver and her beak of
    hammered steel ;
The leg-bar chafed the ankle, and we gasped
    for cooler air,
But no galley on the water with our galley
    could compare !

Our bulkheads bulged with cotton and our
    masts were stepped in gold—
We ran a mighty merchandise of niggers in
    the hold;
The white foam spun behind us, and the
    black shark swam below,
As we gripped the kicking sweep-head and
    we made that galley go.

It was merry in the galley, for we revelled
    now and then—
If they wore us down like cattle, faith, we
    fought and loved like men !

As we snatched her through the water, so
we snatched a minute's bliss,
And the mutter of the dying never spoiled
the lovers' kiss.

Our women and our children toiled beside
us in the dark—
They died, we filed their fetters, and we
heaved them to the shark—
We heaved them to the fishes, but so fast
the galley sped,
We had only time to envy, for we could not
mourn our dead.

Bear witness, once my comrades, what a
hard-bit gang were we—
The servants of the sweep-head, but the
masters of the sea!
By the hands that drove her forward as she
plunged and yawed and sheered,
Woman, Man, or God, or Devil, was there
anything we feared?

Was it storm? Our fathers faced it, and a
wilder never blew;
Earth that waited for the wreckage watched
the galley struggle through.

Burning noon or choking midnight, Sick-
 ness, Sorrow, Parting, Death?
Nay, our very babes would mock you, had
 they time for idle breath.

But to-day I leave the galley, and another
 takes my place;
There's my name upon the deck-beam—let
 it stand a little space.
I am free—to watch my messmates beating
 out to open main,
Free of all that Life can offer—save to han-
 dle sweep again.

By the brand upon my shoulder, by the gall
 of clinging steel,
By the welt the whips have left me, by the
 scars that never heal;
By eyes grown old with staring through the
 sun-wash on the brine.
I am paid in full for service—would that
 service still were mine!

Yet they talk of times and seasons and of
 woe the years bring forth,
Of our galley swamped and shattered in the
 rollers of the North.

When the niggers break the hatches, and the
　　decks are gay with gore,
And a craven-hearted pilot crams her crash-
　　ing on the shore.

She will need no half-mast signal, minute-
　　gun, or rocket-flare,
When the cry for help goes seaward, she
　　will find her servants there.
Battered chain-gangs of the orlop, grizzled
　　drafts of years gone by,
To the bench that broke their manhood,
　　they shall lash themselves and die.

Hale and crippled, young and aged, paid,
　　deserted, shipped away—
Palace, cot, and lazaretto shall make up the
　　tale that day,
When the skies are black above them, and
　　the decks ablaze beneath,
And the top-men clear the raffle with their
　　clasp-knives in their teeth.

It may be that Fate will give me life and
　　leave to row once more—
Set some strong man free for fighting as I
　　take awhile his oar.

But to-day I leave the galley. Shall I curse
    her service then ?
God be thanked—whate'er comes after, I
    have lived and toiled with Men !

The Explanation.

LOVE and Death once ceased their strife
At the Tavern of Man's Life.
Called for wine, and threw—alas !—
Each his quiver on the grass.
When the bout was o'er they found
Mingled arrows strewed the ground.
Hastily they gathered then
Each the loves and lives of men.
Ah, the fateful dawn deceived !
Mingled arrows each one sheaved :
Death's dread armory was stored
With the shafts he most abhorred :
Love's light quiver groaned beneath
Venom-headed darts of Death.
Thus it was they wrought our woe
At the Tavern long ago.
Tell me, do our masters know,
Loosing blindly as they fly,
Old men love while young men die?

The Conundrum of the Workshops.

WHEN the flush of a new-born sun fell first
    on Eden's green and gold,   .
Our father Adam sat under the Tree and
    scratched with a stick in the mould;
And the first rude sketch that the world
    had seen was joy to his mighty heart,
Till the Devil whispered behind the leaves:
    "It's pretty, but is it art?"

Wherefore he called to his wife, and fled to
    fashion his work anew—
The first of his race who cared a fig for the
    first, most dread review;
And he left his lore to the use of his sons—
    and that was a glorious gain
When the Devil chuckled: "Is it art?" in
    the ear of the branded Cain.

They builded a tower to shiver the sky and
    wrench the stars apart,
Till the Devil grunted behind the bricks:
    "It's striking, but is it art?"

The stone was dropped by the quarry-side,
　　and the idle derrick swung,
While each man talked of the aims of art,
　　and each in an alien tongue.

They fought and they talked in the north
　　and the south, they talked and they fought
　　in the west,
Till the waters rose on the jabbering land,
　　and the poor Red Clay had rest—
Had rest till the dank black-canvas dawn
　　when the dove was preened to start,
And the Devil bubbled below the keel:
　·" It's human, but is it art?"

The tale is old as the Eden Tree—as new
　　as the new-cut tooth—
For each man knows ere his lip-thatch
　　grows he is master of art and truth ;
And each man hears as the twilight nears,
　　to the beat of his dying heart,
The Devil drum on the darkened pane:
　" You did it, but was it art "

We have learned to whittle the Eden Tree
　　to the shape of a surplice-peg,
We have learned to bottle our parents twain
　　in the yolk of an addled egg,

We know that the tail must wag the dog, as
    the horse is drawn by the cart;
But the Devil whoops, as he whooped of old:
    "It's clever, but is it art?"

When the flicker of London sun falls faint
    on the club-room's green and gold,
The sons of Adam sit them down and scratch
    with their pens in the mould—
They scratch with their pens in the mould
    of their graves, and the ink and the an-
    guish start
When the Devil mutters behind the leaves:
    "It's pretty, but is it art?"

Now, if we could win to the Eden Tree
    where the four great rivers flow,
And the wreath of Eve is red on the turf as
    she left it long ago,
And if we could come when the sentry slept,
    and softly scurry through,
By the favor of God we might know as much
    —as our father Adam knew.

The Gift of the Sea.

THE dead child lay in the shroud,
   And the widow watched beside ;
And her mother slept, and the Channel
   swept
The gale in the teeth of the tide.

But the widow laughed at all.
   " I have lost my man in the sea,
And the child is dead. Be still," she said,
   " What more can ye do to me ?"

And the widow watched the dead,
   And the candle gutted low,
And she tried to sing the Passing Song
   That bids the poor soul go.

And " Mary take you now," she sang,
   " That lay against my heart."
And " Mary smooth your crib to-night,"
   But she could not say " Depart."

Then came a cry from the sea,
  But the sea-rime blinded the glass,
And "Heard ye nothing, mother?" she
    said;
  " 'Tis the child that waits to pass."

And the nodding mother sighed. ·
  " 'Tis a lambing ewe in the whin,
For why should the christened soul cry out,
  That never knew of sin?"

"Oh, feet I have held in my hand,
  Oh, hands at my heart to catch,
How should they know the road to go,
  And how should they lift the latch?"

They laid a sheet to the door,
  With the little quilt atop,
That it might not hurt from the cold or the
    dirt,
  But the crying would not stop.

The widow lifted the latch
  And strained her eyes to see,
And opened the door on the bitter shore
  To let the soul go free.

There was neither glimmer nor ghost,
  There was neither spirit nor spark,
And " Heard ye nothing, mother ?" she said,
  " 'Tis crying for me in the dark."

And the nodding mother sighed.
  " 'Tis sorrow makes ye dull;
Have ye yet to learn the cry of the tern,
  Or the wail of the wind-blown gull ?"

" The terns are blown inland,
  The gray gull follows the plough.
'Twas never a bird the voice I heard,
  O mother, I hear it now !"

" Lie still, dear lamb, lie still;
  The child is passed from harm,
'Tis the ache in your breast that broke your
    rest,
  And the feel of an empty arm."

She puts her mother aside,
  " In Mary's name let be !
For the peace of my soul I must go," she
    said,
  And she went to the calling sea.

In the heel of the wind-bit pier,
 Where the twisted weed was piled,
She came to the life she had missed **by an**
  hour,
 For she came to a little child.

She laid it into her breast,
 And back to her mother she came,
But it would not feed, and it would not heed,
 Though she gave it her own child's name.

And the dead child dripped on her breast,
 And her own in the shroud lay stark;
And, "God forgive us, mother," she said,
 "We let it die in the dark!"

Evarra and His Gods.

Read here,
This is the story of Evarra—man—
Maker of Gods in lands beyond the sea.
Because the city gave him of her gold,
Because the caravans brought turquoises,
Because his life was sheltered by the King,
So that no man should maim him, none
    should steal,
Or break his rest with babble in the streets
When he was weary after toil, he made
An image of his God in gold and pearl,
With turquoise diadem and human eyes,
A wonder in the sunshine, known afar
And worshipped by the King; but, drunk
    with pride,
Because the city bowed to him for God,
He wrote above the shrine: "*Thus Gods*
    are made,
And whoso makes them otherwise shall die."
And all the city praised him. . . . Then
    he died.

Read here the story of Evarra—man—
Maker of Gods in lands beyond the sea.
  Because his city had no wealth to give,
  Because the caravans were spoiled afar,
  Because his life was threatened by the
    King,
  So that all men despised him in the streets,
  He hacked the living rock, with sweat and
    tears,
  And reared a God against the morning-
    gold,
  A terror in the sunshine, seen afar,
  And worshipped by the King; but, drunk
    with pride,
  Because the city fawned to bring him back,
  He carved upon the plinth: "*Thus Gods*
    are made,
And whoso makes them otherwise shall die."
  And all the people praised him. . . . Then
    he died.

Read here the story of Evarra—man—
Maker of Gods in lands beyond the sea.
  Because he lived among a simple folk,
  Because his village was between the hills,
  Because he smeared his cheeks with blood
    of ewes,

He cut an idol from a fallen pine,
Smeared blood upon its cheeks, and
wedged a shell
Above its brows for eye, and gave it hair
Of trailing moss, and plaited straw for
crown.
And all the village praised him for this
craft,
And brought him butter, honey, milk, and
curds.
Wherefore, because the shoutings drove
him mad,
He scratched upon that log: "*Thus Gods
are made,
And whoso makes them otherwise shall die.*"
And all the people praised him. . . . Then
he died.

Read here the story of Evarra—man—
Maker of Gods in lands beyond the sea.
Because his God decreed one clot of blood
Should swerve a hair's-breadth from the
pulse's path,
And chafe his brain, Evarra mowed alone,
Rag-wrapped, among the cattle in the fields,
Counting his fingers, jesting with the trees,
And mocking at the mist, until his God

Drove him to labor. Out of dung and
    horns
Dropped in the mire he made a mon-
    strous God,
Abhorrent, shapeless, crowned with plan-
    tain tufts.
And when the cattle lowed at twilight-
    time,
He dreamed it was the clamor of lost
    crowds,
And howled among the beasts: "*Thus
  Gods are made,*
And whoso makes them otherwise shall die."
Thereat the cattle bellowed. . . . Then
    he died.

Yet at the last he came to Paradise,
And found his own four Gods, and that
    he wrote;
And marvelled, being very near to God,
What oaf on earth had made his toil God's
    law,
Till God said, mocking: "Mock not. These
    be thine."
Then cried Evarra: "I have sinned!"—
    "Not so.
If thou hadst written otherwise, thy Gods

Had rested in the mountain and the mine,
And I were poorer by four wondrous
    Gods,
And thy more wondrous law, Evarra.
    Thine,
Servant of shouting crowds and lowing
    kine."
Thereat with laughing mouth, but tear-wet
    eyes,
Evarra cast his Gods from Paradise.

This is the story of Evarra—man—
Maker of Gods in lands beyond the sea.

Public Waste.

WALPOLE talks of "a man and his price."
List to a ditty queer—
The sale of a Deputy-Acting-Vice-
Resident-Engineer,
Bought like a bullock, hoof and hide,
By the Little Tin Gods on the Mountain Side.

BY the Laws of the Family Circle 'tis writ-
ten in letters of brass
That only a Colonel from Chatham can man-
age the Railways of State,
Because of the gold on his breeks, and the
subjects wherein he must pass;
Because in all matters that deal not with
Railways his knowledge is great.

Now Exeter Battleby Tring had labored
from boyhood to eld
On the lines of the East and the West, and
eke of the North and South;
Many Lines had he built and surveyed—im-
portant the posts which he held;
And the Lords of the Iron Horse were dumb
when he opened his mouth.

(202)

Black as the raven his garb, and his heresies
    jettier still—
Hinting that Railways required lifetimes of
    study and knowledge ;
Never clanked sword by his side—Vauban
    he knew not, nor drill—
Nor was his name on the list of the men who
    had passed through the " College."

Wherefore the Little Tin Gods harried their
    little tin souls,
Seeing he came not from Chatham, jingled
    no spurs at his heels,
Knowing that, nevertheless, was he first on
    the Government rolls
For the billet of " Railway Instructor to Lit-
    tle Tin Gods on Wheels."

Letters not seldom they wrote him, " having
    the honor to state,"
It would be better for all men if he were laid
    on the shelf :
Much would accrue to his bank-book, and
    he consented to wait
Until the Little Tin Gods built him a berth
    for himself.

"Special, well-paid, and exempt from the
　Law of the Fifty and Five,
Even to Ninety and Nine"—these were the
　terms of the pact:
Thus did the Little Tin Gods (long may
　Their Highnesses thrive!)
Silence his mouth with rupees, keeping their
　Circle intact;

Appointing a Colonel from Chatham who
　managed the Bhamo State line,
(The which was one mile and one furlong—
　a guaranteed twenty-inch gauge).
So Exeter Battleby Tring consented his
　claims to resign,
And died, on four thousand a month, in the
　ninetieth year of his age.

The Last Department.

TWELVE hundred million men are spread
About this Earth, and I and You
Wonder, when You and I are dead,
What will those luckless millions do?

"NONE whole or clean," we cry, "or free
  from stain
Of favor." Wait awhile, till we attain
  The Last Department, where no fraud nor
  fools,
Nor grade nor greed, shall trouble us again.

Fear, Favor or Affection—what are these
To the grim Head who claims our services?
  I never knew a wife or interest yet
Delay that *pukka* step, miscalled " decease;"

When leave, long over-due, none can deny·
When idleness of all Eternity
  Becomes our furlough, and the marigold
Our thriftless, bullion-minting Treasury.

Transferred to the Eternal Settlement,
Each in his straight, wood-scantled office
  pent,
  No longer Brown reverses Smith's appeals,
Or Jones records his Minute of Dissent.

And One, long since a pillar of the Court,
As mud between the beams thereof is
 wrought;
 And One who wrote on phosphates for the
  crops
Is subject-matter of his own Report.

(These be the glorious ends whereto we
 pass—
Let Him who Is, go call on Him who Was;
 And He shall see the *mallie* steals the slab
For currie-grinder, and for goats the grass.)

A breath of wind, a Border bullet's flight,
A draught of water, or a horse's fright—
 The droning of the fat *Sheristadar*
Ceases, the punkah stops, and falls the night

For you or Me. Do those who live decline
The step that offers, or their work resign?
 Trust me, To-day's Most Indispensables,
Five hundred men can take your place or
 mine.

Possibilities.

AY, lay him 'neath the Simla pine—
   A fortnight fully to be missed,
   Behold, we lose our fourth at whist,
A chair is vacant where we dine.

His place forgets him; other men
   Have bought his ponies, guns, and traps.
   His fortune is the Great Perhaps
And that cool rest-house down the glen,

Whence he shall hear, as spirits may,
   Our mundane revel on the height,
   Shall watch each flashing *'rickshaw*-light
Sweep on to dinner, dance, and play.

Benmore shall woo him to the ball
   With lighted rooms and braying band,
   And he shall hear and understand
" *Dream Faces* " better than us all.

For, think you, as the vapors flee
   Across Sanjaolie after rain,
   His soul may climb the hill again
To each old field of victory.

Unseen, who women held so dear,
   The strong man's yearning to his kind
   Shall shake at most the window-blind,
Or dull awhile the card-room's cheer.

In his own place of power unknown,
   His Light o' Love another's flame,
   His dearest pony galloped lame,
And he an alien and alone.

Yet may he meet with many a friend—
   Shrewd shadows, lingering long unseen
   Among us when "*God save the Queen*"
Shows even "extras" have an end.

And, when we leave the heated room,
   And, when at four the lights expire.
   The crew shall gather round the fire
And mock our laughter in the gloom.

Talk as we talked, and they ere death—
   First wanly, dance in ghostly wise,
   With ghosts of tunes for melodies,
And vanish at the morning's breath.

In Springtime.

MY garden blazes brightly with the rose-
 bush and the peach,
 And the *koil* sings above it, in the *siris* by
  the well,
From the creeper-covered trellis comes the
 squirrel's chattering speech,
 And the blue-jay screams and nutters
  where the cherry *sat-bhai* dwell.
But the rose has lost its fragance, and the
 koil's note is strange;
 I am sick of endless sunshine, sick of
  blossom-burdened bough.
Give me back the leafless woodlands where
 the winds of Springtime range—
 Give me back one day in England, for it's
  Spring in England now!
Through the pines the gusts are booming,
 o'er the brown fields blowing chill,
 From the furrow of the ploughshare
  streams the fragrance of the loam,

And the hawk nests on the cliff-side and the
    jackdaw in the hill,
    And my heart is back in England mid the
    sights and sounds of Home.
But the garland of the sacrifice this wealth
    of rose and peach is;
    Ah! *koil*, little *koil*, singing on the *siris*
    bough,
In my ears the knell of exile your ceaseless
    bell-like speech is—
    Can *you* tell me aught of England or of
    Spring in England now?

A Ballade of Jakko Hill.

ONE moment bid the horses wait, ·
   Since tiffin is not laid till three,
Below the upward path and straignt
   You climbed a year ago with me.
Love came upon us suddenly
   And loosed—an idle hour to kill—
A headless, armless armory
   That smote us both on Jakko Hill.

Ah Heaven! we would wait and wait
   Through Time and to Eternity!
Ah Heaven! we could conquer Fate
   With more than Godlike constancy!
I cut the date upon a tree—
   Here stand the clumsy figures still:—
" 10–7–85, A.D."
   Damp with the mist on Jakko Hill.

What came of high resolve and great,
   And until Death fidelity?
Whose horse is waiting at your·gate?
   Whose 'rickshaw-wheels ride over me?

No Saint's, I swear; and—let me see
  To-night what names your programme
    fill—
We drift asunder merrily,
  As drifts the mist on Jakko Hill!

L'ENVOI.

Princess, behold our ancient state
  Has clean departed; and we see
'Twas Idleness we took for Fate
  That bound light bonds on you and **me.**
Amen! Here ends the comedy
  Where it began in all good will;
Since Love and Leave together flee
  As driven mist on Jakko Hill!

The Plea of the Simla Dancers.

Too late, alas! the song
To remedy the wrong;—
The rooms are taken from us, swept and garnished for their
fate.
But these tear-besprinkled pages
Shall attest to future ages
That we cried against the crime of it—too late, alas! too late!

"WHAT have *we* ever done to bear this
 grudge?"
Was there no room save only in Benmore
For docket, *duftar*, and for office drudge,
 That you usurp our smoothest dancing
 floor?
Must babus do their work on polished teak?
 Are ball-rooms fittest for the ink you spill?
Was there no other cheaper house to seek?
 You might have left them all at Straw-
 berry Hill.

We never harmed you! Innocent our guise,
 Dainty our shining feet, our voices low;
And we revolved to divers melodies,
 And we were happy but a year ago.·
To-night, the moon that watched our light-
 some wiles—

That beamed upon us through the deo-
    dars—   .
Is wan with gazing on official files,
    And desecrating desks disgust the stars.

Nay! by the memory of tuneful nights—
    Nay! by the witchery of flying feet—
Nay! by the glamour of fordone delights—
    By all things merry, musical, and meet—
By wine that sparkled, and by sparkling
    eyes—
    By wailing waltz—by reckless gallop's
        strain—   .
By dim verandas and by soft replies,
    Give us our ravished ball-room back
        again!

Or—hearken to the curse we lay on you!
    The ghosts of waltzes shall perplex your
        brain,
And murmurs of past merriment pursue
    Your 'wildered clerks that they indite in
        vain;
And, when you count your poor Provincial
    millions,
    The only figures that your pen shall
        frame

Shall be the figures of dear, dear cotillions
  Danced out in tumult long before you
    came.

Yea! "*See Saw*" shall upset your estimates,
  "*Dream Faces*" shall your heavy heads
    bemuse,
Because your hand, unheeding, desecrates
  Our temple; fit for higher, worthier use.
And all the long verandas, eloquent
  With echoes of a score of Simla years,
Shall plague you with unbidden sentiment—
  Babbling of kisses, laughter, love, and
    tears.

So shall you mazed amid old memories
    stand,
  So shall you toil, and shall accomplish
    nought,
And ever in your ears a phantom Band
  Shall blare away the staid official thought.
Wherefore—and ere this awful curse be
    spoken,
  Cast out your swarthy sacrilegious train,
And give—ere dancing cease and hearts be
    broken—
Give us our ravished ball-room back again!

Two Months.

In June.

NO hope, no change! The clouds have
    shut us in,
And through the cloud the sullen Sun
    strikes down
Full on the bosom of the tortured Town.

Till Night falls heavy as remembered sin
That will not suffer sleep or thought of
    ease.
  And, hour on hour, the dry-eyed Moon
    in spite
  Glares through the haze and mocks with
    watery light
The torment of the uncomplaining trees.

(216)

Far off, the Thunder bellows her despair
To echoing Earth, thrice parched. The
    lightnings fly
In vain. No help the heaped-up clouds
    afford,
But wearier weight of burdened, burning
    air.
What truce with Dawn? Look, from the
    aching sky,
Day stalks, a tyrant with a flaming sword!

Two Months.

In September.

AT dawn there was a murmur in the trees,
  A ripple on the tank, and in the air
  Presage of coming coolness—everywhere
A voice of prophecy upon the breeze.
Up leapt the Sun and smote the dust to
    gold,
    And strove to parch anew the heedless
    land,
All impotently, as a King grown old
  Wars for the Empire crumbling 'neath
    his hand,   .

One after one, the lotos-petals fell,
Beneath the onslaught of the rebel year
In mutiny against a furious sky;
And far-off Winter whispered:— "It is
    well!
"Hot Summer dies. Behold your help is
    near,
"For when men's need is sorest, then
    come I."

(218)

The Moon of Other Days.

BENEATH the deep verandah's shade,
   When bats begin to fly,
I sit me down and watch—alas
   Another evening die.
Blood-red behind the sere *ferash*
   She rises through the haze.
Sainted Diana! can that be
   The Moon of Other Days!

Ah! shade of little Kitty Smith,
   Sweet Saint of Kensington!
Say, was it ever thus at Home
   The Moon of August shone,
When arm in arm we wandered long
   Through Putney's evening haze,
And Hammersmith was Heaven beneath
   The Moon of Other Days?

But Wandle's stream is Sutlej now,
   And Putney's evening haze
The dust that half a hundred kine
   Before my window raise.
Unkempt, unclean, athwart the mist
   The seething city looms,
In place of Putney's golden gorse
   The sickly *babul* blooms.

Glare down, old Hecate, through the dust
   And bid the pie-dog yell,
Draw from the drain its typhoid germ,
   From each bazar its smell;
Yea, suck the fever from the tank
   And sap my strength therewith :
Thank Heaven, you show a smiling face
   To little Kitty Smith !

The Fall of Jock Gillespie.

THIS fell when dinner-time was done—
  'Twixt the first an' the second rub—
That oor mon Jock cam' hame again
  To his rooms ahint the Club.

An' syne he laughed, an' syne he sang,
  An' syne we thocht him fou,
An' syne he trumped his partner's trick,
  An' garred his partner rue.

Then up and spake an elder mon,
  That held the Spade its Ace—
"God save the lad! Whence comes the
    licht
  " That wimples on his face?"

An' Jock he sniggered, an' Jock he
    smiled,
  An' ower the card-brim wunk:—
"I'm a' too fresh fra' the stirrup-peg,
  " May be that I am drunk."

(221)

" There's whusky brewed in Galashiels,
    "An' L. L. L. forbye ;
" But never liquor lit the low
    " That keeks fra' oot your eye.

" There's a thrid o' hair on your dress-
        coat breast,
    "Aboon the heart a wee? "
" Oh ! that is fra' the lang-haired Skye
    " That slobbers ower me."

"Oh ! lang-haired Skyes are lovin' beasts,
    "An' terrier dogs are fair,
" But never yet was terrier born,
    " Wi' ell-lang gowden hair !

" There's a smirch o' pouther on your
        breast,
    " Below the left lappel? "
" Oh ! that is fra' my auld cigar,
    " Whenas the stump-end fell."

" Mon Jock, ye smoke the Trichi coarse,
    " For ye are short o' cash.
"An' best Havannahs couldna leave,
    " Sae white an' pure an ash.

' This nicht ye stopped a story braid,
 "An' stopped it wi' a curse—
' Last nicht ye told that tale yoursel,
 "An capped it wi' a worse !

'Oh ! we're no fou ! Oh ! we're no fou !
 " But plainly we can ken
' Ye're fallin', fallin', fra' the band
 " O' cantie single men ! "

An' it fell when *sirris*-shaws were sere,
 An' the nichts were lang and mirk,
In braw new breeks, wi' a gowden ring,
 Oor Jockie gaed to the Kirk.

The Rupaiyat of Omar Kal'vin.

[Allowing for the difference 'twixt prose and rhymed exaggeration, this ought to reproduce the sense of what Sir A   told the nation some time ago, when the Government struck from our incomes two per cent.]

NOW the New Year, reviving last Year's Debt,
The Thoughtful Fisher casteth wide his Net ;
  So I with begging Dish and ready Tongue
Assail all Men for all that I can get.

Imports indeed are gone with all their Dues—
Lo! Salt a Lever that I dare not use,
  Nor may I ask the Tillers in Bengal—
Surely my Kith and Kin will not refuse

Pay—and I promise by the Dust of Spring,
Retrenchment. If my promises can bring
  Comfort, Ye have Them now a thousand-fold—
By Allah! I will promise *Anything!*

(224)

Indeed, indeed, Retrenchment oft before
I swore—but did I mean it when I swore?'
  And then, and then, We wandered to
    the Hills,
And so the Little Less became Much More..

Whether at Boileaugunge or Babylon,
I know not how the wretched Thing is
    done,
  The Items of Receipt grow surely small;.
The Items of Expense mount one by one.

I cannot help it. What have I to do
With One and Five, or Four, or Three, or
    Two?
  Let Scribes spit Blood and Sulphur as'
    they please,
Or Statesmen call me foolish—Heed not
    you.

Behold, I promise—Anything You will.
Behold, I greet you with an empty Till—
  -Ah! Fellow-Sinners, of your Charity
Seek not the Reason of the Dearth but fill.

For if I sinned and fell, where lies the Gain
Of Knowledge? Would it ease you of
    your Pain
  To know the tangled Threads of Reve-
    nue,
I ravel deeper in a hopeless Skein?

"Who hath not Prudence"—what was it
    I said,
Of Her who paints her Eyes and tires Her
    Head,
  And jibes and mocks the People in the
    Street,
And fawns upon them for Her thriftless
    Bread?

Accursed is She of Eve's daughters—She
Hath cast off Prudence, and Her End shall
    be
  Destruction . . . . Brethren, of your
    Bounty grant
Some portion of your daily Bread to *Me*.

What Happened.

HURREE Chunder Mookerjee, pride of
    Bow Bazar,
Owner of a native press, "Barrishter-at-
    Lar,"
Waited on the Government with a claim
    to wear
Sabres by the bucketful, rifles by the pair.

Then the Indian Government winked a
    wicked wink,
Said to Chunder Mookerjee: "Stick to
    pen and ink.
They are safer implements, but, if you
    insist,
We will let you carry arms wheresoe'er
    you list."

Hurree Chunder Mookerjee sought the
    gunsmith and
Bought the tubes of Lancaster, Ballard,
    Dean, and Bland,

Bought a shiny bowie-knife, bought a
　　town-made sword,
Jingled like a carriage-horse when he went
　　abroad.

But the Indian Government, always keen
　　to please,
Also gave permission to horrid men like
　　these—
Yar Mahommed Yusufzai, down to kill or
　　steal,
Chimbu Singh from Bikaneer, Tantia the
　　Bhil.

Killar Khan the Marri chief, Jowar Singh
　　the Sikh,
Nubbee Baksh Punjabi Jat, Abdul Huq
　　Rafiq—
He was a Wahabi; last, little Boh Hla-oo
Took advantage of the act—took a Snider
　　too.

They were unenlightened men, Ballard
　　knew them not,
They procured their swords and guns
　　chiefly on the spot,

And the lore of centuries, plus a hundred
    fights,
Made them slow to disregard one another's
    rights.

With a unanimity dear to patriot hearts
All those hairy gentlemen out of foreign
    parts
Said: " The good old days are back—let
    us go to war ! "
Swaggered down the Grand Trunk Road
    into Bow Bazar.

Nubbee Baksh Punjabi Jat found a hide-
    bound flail,
Chimbu Singh from Bikaneer oiled his
    Tonk jezail,
Yar Mahommed Yusufzai spat and grinned
    with glee
As he ground the butcher-knife of the
    Khyberee.

Jowar Singh the Sikh procured sabre, quoit
    and mace,
Abdul Huq, Wahabi, took the dagger from
    its place,

While amid the jungle-grass danced and
    grinned and jabbered
Little Boh Hla-oo and cleared the dah-
    blade from the scabbard.

What became of Mookerjee? Soothly, who
    can say?
Yar Mahommed only grins in a nasty
    way,
Jowar Singh is reticent, Chimbu Singh is
    mute,
But the belts of all of them simply bulge
    with loot.

What became of Ballard's guns? Afghans
    black and grubby
Sell them for their silver weight to the
    men of Pubbi;
And the shiny bowie-knife and the town-
    made sword are
Hanging in a Marri camp just across the
    Border.

What became of Mookerjee? Ask Mahom-
    med Yar
Prodding Siva's sacred bull down the Bow
    Bazar.

Speak to placid Nubbee Baksh—question
  land and sea—
Ask the Indian Congress men—only don't
  ask me !

Study of an Elevation, in Indian Ink.

This ditty is a string of lies.
But—how the deuce did Gubbins rise?

POTIPHAR Gubbins, C. E.,
Stands at the top of the tree;
And I muse in my bed on the reasons that
led
To the hoisting of Potiphar G.

Potiphar Gubbins, C. E.,
Is seven years junior to Me;
Each bridge that he makes either buckles
or breaks,
And his work is as rough as he.

Potiphar Gubbins, C. E.,
Is coarse as a chimpanzee;
And I can't understand why you gave him
your hand,
Lovely Mehitabel Lee.

(232)

Potiphar Gubbins, C. E.,
Is dear to the Powers that Be;
For They bow and They smile in an affable
style,
Which is seldom accorded to Me.

Potiphar Gubbins, C. E.,
Is certain as certain can be
Of a highly paid post which is claimed by
a host
Of seniors—including Me.

Careless and lazy is he,
Greatly inferior to Me.
What is the spell that you manage so well
Commonplace Potiphar G. ?

Lovely Mehitabel Lee,
Let me inquire of thee,
Should I have riz to what Potiphar is
Hadst thou been mated to Me ?

The Vampire.

[The verses—as suggested by the painting by Philip Burne-Jones, first exhibited at the new gallery in London in 1897.]

A FOOL there was and he made his prayer
(Even as you and I !)
To a rag and a bone and a hank of hair
(We called her the woman who did not
    care),
But the fool he called her his lady fair
(Even as you and I !)

Oh the years we waste and the tears we
    waste
And the work of our head and hand,
Belong to the woman who did not know
(And now we know that she never could
    know)
And did not understand.

(234)

A fool there was and his goods he spent
(Even as you and I !)
Honor and faith and a sure intent
(And it wasn't the least what the lady
meant),
But a fool must follow his natural bent
(Even as you and I !)

Oh the toil we lost and the spoil we lost
And the excellent things we planned,
Belong to the woman who didn't know
why
(And now we know she never knew
why)
And did not understand.

The fool was stripped to his foolish hide
(Even as you and I !)
Which she might have seen when she
threw him aside—
(But it isn't on record the lady tried)
So some of him lived but the most of him
died—
(Even as you and I !)

And it isn't the shame and it isn't the
  blame
That stings like a white hot brand.
It's coming to know that she never knew
  why
(Seeing at last she could never know why)
And never could understand.

Recessional.

A Victorian Ode.

GOD of our fathers, known of old—
Lord of our far-flung battle line—
Beneath whose awful hand we hold
Dominion over palm and pine—
Lord God of Hosts, be with us yet,
Lest we forget—lest we forget!

The tumult and the shouting dies—
The Captains and the Kings depart—
Still stands Thine ancient sacrifice,
An humble and a contrite heart,
Lord God of Hosts, be with us yet,
Lest we forget—lest we forget!

Far-called our navies melt away—
On dune and headland sinks the fire—
Lo, all our pomp of yesterday
Is one with Nineveh and Tyre!
Judge of the Nations, spare us yet,
Lest we forget—lest we forget!

If, drunk with sight of power, we loose
Wild tongues that have not thee in awe—
Such boasting as the Gentiles use,
Or lesser breeds without the Law—
Lord God of Hosts, be with us yet,
Lest we forget—lest we forget!

For heathen heart that puts her trust
In reeking tube and iron shard—
All valiant dust that builds on dust,
And guarding calls not Thee to guard.
For frantic boast and foolish word,
Thy Mercy on Thy People Lord!

Amen.

L'Envoi.

(To whom it may concern.)

THE smoke upon your Altar dies,
   The flowers decay,
The Goddess of your sacrifice
   Has flown away.
What profit then to sing or slay
The sacrifice from day to day?

"We know the Shrine is void," they said,
   " The Goddess flown—
Yet wreaths are on the Altar laid—
   The Altar-Stone
Is black with fumes of sacrifice,
Albeit She has fled our eyes.

" For, it may be, if still we sing
   And tend the Shrine,
Some Deity on wandering wing
   May there incline;
And, finding all in order meet,
Stay while we worship at Her feet."

Glossary.

AFRIDIS, . . .	An Afghán clan west and south of Peshawar.
ALLAH, . . .	The Mahommedan name for God.
ANNANDALE, .	A valley near Simla—the Simla Racecourse, etc.
AVATAR, . . .	An incarnation on earth of a divine Being.
BABU, ...	A title such as "Mr.," used frequently to signify a Bengali clerk.
BABUL, . . .	A small thorny mimosa jungle tree, blossoms profusely a bright yellow tassel-like flower, like a bullet, and with a fragrance resembling that of the wallflower.
BANDAR, . . .	A monkey.
BAZUGAR, . .	One who exhibits feats of activity.
BEGUM, . . .	A lady, a queen.
BENMORE, . .	The old Simla Assembly Rooms.
BHAMO, . . .	A district in Upper Burma.
BIKANEER, . .	A state in Rajputana.
BOH, ...	A captain in the Burmese native army.
BOILEAUGUNGE,	A suburb of Simla, named after General Boileau.
BOW BAZAR, .	One of the principal bazars in Calcutta.
BRAHMIN, . .	A member of the priestly caste.
BRINJAREE, . .	The Brinjarees of the Deccan are dealers in grain and salt.
BUKHSHI, . .	A paymaster in the Anglo-Indian army.

(240)

BUL-BUL, . . .	The Persian nightingale.
BUNNIA, . . .	A corn and seed merchant or dealer.
BURSAT, . . .	The rains, which set in about the middle of June—the first burst of them is known as the "chota bursat," or small rains—after which there is generally a break before the regular monsoon sets in.
BURSATI, . . .	A disease to which horses are liable during the rains.
BYLE, ...	A bullock.
CHARNOCK, . .	Job Charnock, the founder of Calcutta.
CHOTA BURSAT, see "bursat."	
COLLINGA, . .	One of the bazars in Calcutta where most of the demi-monde resided.
COOLY, . . .	A hired laborer, or burden-carrier.
DAH BLADE, .	"Dah" is a short Burmese sword.
DAK, ...	"Post," *i.e.*, properly, transport by relays of men and horses.
DAK-BUNGALOW,	A rest house for travellers.
DARJEELING, .	A Sanitarium in the Himalaya. The summer seat of the Bengal Government.
DEODARS, . .	The "Cedrus deodarus" of the Himalaya.
DIBS, ...	A slang term for money—rupees.
DOM, ...	The name of a very low caste representing some old aboriginal race spread all over India. In many places they perform such offices as carrying dead bodies, removing carrion, etc.
DUFTAR, . . .	Book, Journal, Record—sometimes used instead of "duftar khana" for "the office."
DUSTOORIE, . .	A commission on the money passing in any cash transaction.

DYKES, . . . A firm of coach builders in Calcutta.

FERASH (faras), a species of date-tree.

FULTAH, . . . A village in Bengal, situated on the Hughli; also an anchorage for vessels.

GARDEN REACH, The reach or bend forming the entrance to the Port of Calcutta —so called on account of the fine garden residences which at one time lined the banks of the river at this part.

GHAT, ... A mountain pass, landing place, or ferry.

GHI, ... Boiled or clarified butter.

HAFIZ, . . . A guardian, governor, preserver

HAMILTON, . . Hamilton & Co., jewellers.

HOOKUM, . . An order, command.

HOWRAH, . . A large town opposite Calcutta.

HUGHLI (or Hooghly). One of the principal rivers of Hindustan on which Calcutta is situated.

HURNAI, . . . A pass leading from Baluchistan to Afghanistan.

JAIN, ... The non-Brahminical sect so-called —believed now to represent the earliest heretics of Buddhism, at present chiefly found in the Bombay presidency. The Jains are generally merchants, and some have been men of immense wealth.

JAKKO, . . . A mountain peak in the Punjab— one of the highest of the Himalaya on which Simla is situated.

JAT, ... A tribe among Rajputs.

JAUN BAZAR, . One of the principal bazars in Calcutta.

JEHANNUM, . . Hades, hell.

JEMADAR, . . The second native officer in a company of Sepoys.

JEZAIL, . . . A heavy Afghan rifle, fired with a forked rest.

JINGAL, . . . A small piece of Burmese artillery mounted on a carriage, managed by two men.

JUNGLE, . . . Forest, or other wild growth.

JUTOGH, . . . A military station in the Punjab, at the entrance of Simla.

KAFIR, . . . An unbeliever in the Moslem faith.

KAKAHUTTI, . A village in the Punjab, on the road to Simla from the plains.

KALKA, . . . A villa in the Punjab, at the foot of the Himalaya, on the road from Umballa to Simla.

KEDGEREE, . . A village and police station near the mouth of the Hughlí; also an anchorage for vessels.

KITMUTGARS, . Table servants—a Mahommedan who will also perform the duties of a valet.

KHUD, . . . A precipitous hill side, a deep valley.

KHYRAGHAUT, A halting station near Simla.

KHYBEREE (Khaibari), An Afghan tribe inhabiting the Khaibar pass in Afghanistan.

KOIL, ... The Indian nightingale.

KULLAH, . . A term used generally by Burmese for a western foreigner, a stranger.

KURRUM, . . A mountain pass into Afghanistan from the Punjab.

LAKH, . . . One hundred thousand rupees.

LANGUR, . . . The great white-bearded ape, much patronized by Hindus, and identified with the monkey-god, Huni-

MAG, ...	Natives of Arakan.
MAHRATTA, . .	The name of a famous Hindu race. The British won India from the two Hindu confederacies, the Marathas and the Sikhs.
MALLIE, . . .	A gardener.
MASHOBRA, . .	A village and hill in the Punjab, near Simla.
MICHINI, . . .	A fort in the Punjab.
MLECH, . . .	One without caste.
MOOLTAN, . .	A district in the Punjab.
MARRI (Murree),	A Hill Station and Sanitarium in the Punjab.
MUSTH, . . .	In a state of periodical excitement.
NAT, ...	A term applied to all spiritual beings, angels, elfs, demons, or what not, including the gods of the Hindus.
OCTROI, . . .	A municipal tax.
PADRE, . . .	A priest, clergyman, or minister of the Christian religion.
PEG, ...	A term used for a brandy (or other spirit) and soda.
PELITI, . . .	A well-known confectioner.
PICE, ...	The smallest copper coin—12 pice = 1 anna, 16 annas = 1 rupee.
PUKKA. . . .	Ripe, mature, cooked; and hence substantial, permanent, with many specific applications. One of the most common uses in which the word has become specific is that of brick and mortar in contradistinction to one of inferior material, as of mud, matting, or timber.
PUNJABI, . . .	A native of the Punjab.

PUNKAH, . . A large swinging fan suspended from the ceiling and pulled by a cooly.

QUETTA, . : . A town and cantonment in Baluchistan under British administration.

RAJAH, . . . A native chief.

RAMA, . . . One of the Puranic Deities. The hero of the Sanskrit epic, the Ramáyana.

RANKEN, . . . Ranken & Co., tailors.

'RICKSHAW, . . A contraction of "Jinny rickshaw," a two-wheeled conveyance drawn by a cooly.

RUPAIYAT of Omar Kal'vin, a play on Rubaiyat of Omar Khayyam, signifying (The Poem) connected with rupees of Omar Kal'vin (a late financial member of the Viceroy's Council).

RYOT, ... A tenant of the soil.

SAHIB, . . . A lord, master, companion, gentleman, commonly used to denote a European.

SAMADH, . . . A cenotaph.

SAT-BHAI (lit. the seven brothers), a species of thrush, so called from the birds being gregarious, and usually seven of them are found together.

SHRAI, . . . A place for the accommodation of travellers, a khan, a caravansary.

SHAITANPORE, . A fictitious name for a place. Shaitan signifies the Evil One—pore, a common termination, signifies a city.

SAERISTADAR, . The head ministerial officer of a court, whose duty it is to receive plaints.

SHIKAR, . . . Sport, hunting, chase, prey, game, plunder, perquisites.

SHROFF, . . . A money-changer, a banker.

SIKH, ... A "disciple," the distinctive name of the disciples of Nanak Shah, who in the 16th century established that sect, which eventually rose to warlike predominance in the Punjab, and from which sprung Ranjat Singh, the founder of the brief kingdom of Lahore.

"SIMPKIN," . A Hindustani corruption of the word "champagne."

SIRIS, ... The tree Acacia, a timber tree of moderate size, best known in the Upper Provinces.

SIVA, . . . A Hindu god, the Destroyer and Reproducer, the third person in the Hindu triad.

SOLON, . . A cantonment and hill sanitarium in the Punjab, near Simla.

SUBADAR, . . The chief native officer of a company of Sepoys.

SUNDERBUNDS, . The well-known name of the tract of intersecting creeks and channels, swampy islands and jungles which constitute that part of the Ganges Delta nearest the sea.

SUTLEJ, . . . One of the principal rivers of India.

SUTTEE, . . . The rite of widow-burning.

TAMARISKS, . A graceful, feather-like shrub; is covered with numberless little spikes of small pink flowers when in blossom.

TATIA THE BHIL, A well-known dacoit of the Central Provinces.

TARA DEVI, . One of the Himalaya mountain peaks, near Simla.

THAG, ... A highway robber, garotter.

THANA, . . . A police station.

THAKUR, . . A chief (among Rajputs).

THERMANTIDOTE (heat-antidote), A sort of winnowing machine fitted to a window aperture, and incased in wet tatties so as to drive a current of cooled air into a house during hot dry weather (tatties are screens or mats made of the roots of a fragrant grass).

TONGA, . . . A two-wheeled car drawn by two ponies curricle fashion, used for travelling in the hills.

TONK, ... A state and city in Rájputana.

"TRICHI," . . A contraction of Trichinopoly, a place on the S. E. coast of Hindustan, noted for its cigars—hence "Trichi" denotes a Trichinopoly cigar.

TULWAR, . . . A sabre, used by the Sikhs.

UMBALLA, . . A city and cantonment of the Umballa district, Punjab. Formerly the nearest station on the railway to Simla.

WAHABIS, . . A fanatical Mahommedan sect in South Arcot.

WALER, . . . Horses imported from New South Wales are called "Walers."

YABU, ... A class of small hardy horse which comes from the highland country of Kandahar and Cabul.

YUSUFZAIES, . Pathan tribe in Afghanistan.

ZENANA, . . The apartments of a house in which the women of the family are secluded.

PUBLICATIONS OF
HENRY ALTEMUS COMPANY
PHILADELPHIA

ALTEMUS' ILLUSTRATED VADEMECUM SERIES.

Containing the most popular works of standard authors. HANDY VOLUME, LARGE TYPE editions, with appropriate text and full-page illustrations. Superior paper and printing. Illuminated title pages, etched portraits, and original aquarelle frontispieces in eight colors.

Full cloth, ivory finish, embossed gold and inlaid colors, with side titles, boxed, 40 cents.

...190 **Silas Marner.** *Eliot.*
...191 **Sketch Book, The.** *Irving.*
...192 **Snow Image, The,** *Hawthorne.*
.. 199 **Tales from Shakespeare.** *Lamb.*
...200 **Tanglewood Tales.** *Hawthorne.*
...201 **Tartarin of Tarascon.** *Daudet.*
...202 **Tartarin on the Alps.** *Daudet.*
...203 **Ten Nights in a Bar-Room.** *Arthur.*
...204 **Things Will Take a Turn.** *Harraden.*
...205 **Thoughts.** *Marcus Aurelius.*
...206 **Through The Looking Glass.** *Carroll.*
...207 **Tom Brown's School Days.** *Hughes.*
...2c8 **Treasure Island.** *Stevenson.*
...209 **Twice Told Tales.** *Hawthorne.*
...210 **Two Years Before the Mast.** *Dana.*
...211 **The Merchant of Venice.** *Shakespeare.*
...212 **The Merry Wives of Windsor.**
                                        Shakespeare.
...217 **Uncle Tom's Cabin.** *Stowe.*
.. 218 **Undine.** *Fouque.*
...222 **Vic, the autobiography of a fox-terrier.**
                                        Marsh.
...223 **Vicar of Wakefield.** *Goldsmith.*
...226 **Walden.** *Thoreau.*
...227 **Water-Babies.** *Kingsley.*
...228 **Weird Tales.** *Poe.*
...229 **What is Art.** *Tolstoi.*
...230 **Whittier's Poems, Vol. I.**
...231 **Whittier's Poems, Vol II.**
...232 **Window in Thrums.** *Barrie.*
...233 **Women's Work in the Home.** *Farrar.*
...234 **Wonder Book, A.** *Hawthorne.*
...241 **Yellowplush Papers, The.** *Thackeray.*
...244 **Zoe.** *By author of Laddie, etc.*

ALTEMUS' ILLUSTRATED
ONE SYLLABLE SERIES FOR YOUNG READERS.

Embracing popular works arranged for the young folks in words of one syllable.

Printed from extra large clear type on fine enamelled paper and fully illustrated by famous artists. The handsomest line of books for young children before the public.

Fine English cloth ; handsome, new, original designs. 50 cents.

1. **Æsop's Fables.** 62 illustrations.
2. **A Child's Life of Christ.** 49 illustrations.
3. **A Child's Story of the Bible.** 72 illustrations.
4. **The Adventures of Robinson Crusoe.** 70 illustrations.
5. **Bunyan's Pilgrim's Progress.** 46 illustrations.
6. **Swiss Family Robinson.** 50 illustrations.
7. **Gulliver's Travels.** 50 illustrations.
8. **Bible Stories for Little Children.** 80 illustrations.

ALTEMUS'
YOUNG PEOPLES' LIBRARY.

PRICE, 50 CENTS EACH.

Robinson Crusoe. (Chiefly in words of one syllable.) His life and strange, surprising adventures, with 70 beautiful illustrations by Walter Paget.

Alice's Adventures in Wonderland. With 42 illustrations by John Tenniel. "The most delightful of children's stories. Elegant and delicious nonsense."—"Saturday Review."

Through the Looking-glass and what Alice Found There. A companion to "Alice in Wonderland," with 50 illustrations by John Tenniel.

Bunyan's Pilgrim's Progress. Arranged for young readers. With 50 full-page and text illustrations.

A Child's Story of the Bible. With 72 full-page illustrations.

A Child's Life of Christ. With 49 illustrations. Non-sectarian. Children are early attracted and sweetly riveted by the wonderful Story of the Master from the Manger to the Throne.

Swiss Family Robinson. With 50 illustrations. The father of the family tells the tale of the vicissitudes through which he and his wife and children pass, the wonderful discoveries made and dangers encountered. The book is full of interest and instruction.

Christopher Columbus and the Discovery of America. With 70 illustrations. Every American boy and girl should be acquainted with the story of the life of the great discoverer, with its struggles, adventures and trials.

The Story of Exploration and Discovery in Africa. With 80 illustrations. Records the experiences of adventures and discoveries in developing the "Dark Continent."

The Fables of Æsop. Compiled from the best accepted sources. With 62 illustrations. The fables of Æsop are among the very earliest compositions of this kind, and probably have never been surpassed for point and brevity.

Gulliver's Travels. Adapted for young readers, with 50 illustrations.

Mother Goose's Rhymes, Jingles and Fairy Tales. With 234 illustrations.

Lives of the Presidents of the United States. By Prescott Holmes. With portraits of the Presidents and also of the unsuccessful candidates for the office ; as well as the ablest of the Cabinet officers. Revised and up-to-date.

The Story of Adventure in the Frozen Seas. With 70 illustrations. By Prescott Holmes. The book shows how much can be accomplished by steady perseverance and indomitable pluck.

Illustrated Natural History. By the Rev. J. G. Wood, with 80 illustrations. This author has done more to popularize the study of natural history than any other writer. The illustrations are striking and life-like.

A Child's History of England. By Charles Dickens, with 50 illustrations. Tired of listening to his children memorize the twaddle of old-fashioned English history, the author covered the ground in his own peculiar and happy style for his own children's use. When the work was published its success was instantaneous.

Black Beauty : The Autobiography of a Horse. By Anna Sewell, with 50 illustrations. This work is to the animal kingdom what " Uncle Tom's Cabin " was to the Afro-American.

The Arabian Nights Entertainments. With 130 illustrations. Contains the most favorably known of the stories.

Grimm's Fairy Tales. With 55 illustrations. The tales are a wonderful collection, as interesting, from a literary point of view, as they are delightful as stories.

Flower Fables. By Louisa May Alcott. With numerous illustrations, full-page and text.

A series of very interesting fairy tales by the most charming of American story-tellers.

Andersen's Fairy Tales. By Hans Christian Andersen. With 77 illustrations.

These wonderful tales are not only attractive to the young, but equally acceptable to those of mature years.

Grandfather's Chair ; A History for Youth. By Nathaniel Hawthorne. With 60 illustrations. The story of America from the landing of the Puritans to the acknowledgment without reserve of the Independence of the United States.

Aunt Martha's Corner Cupboard. By Mary and Elizabeth Kirby, with 60 illustrations. Stories about Tea, Coffee, Sugar, Rice and Chinaware, and other accessories of the well-kept Cupboard.

Battles of the War for Independence. By Prescott Holmes, with 70 illustrations. A graphic and full history of the Rebellion of the American Colonies from the yoke and oppression of England. Including also an account of the second war with Great Britain, and the War with Mexico.

Battles of the War for the Union. By Prescott Holmes, with 80 illustrations. A correct and *impartial* account of the greatest civil war in the annals of history. Both of these histories of American wars are a necessary part of the education of all intelligent American boys and girls.

Water Babies. By Charles Kingsley, with 84 illustrations. A charming fairy tale.

Young People's History of the War with Spain. By Prescott Holmes, with 86 illustrations. The story of the war for the freedom of Cuba, arranged for young readers.

Heroes of the United States Navy. By Hartwell James, with 65 illustrations. From the days of the Revolution until the end of the War with Spain.

Military Heroes of the United States. By Hartwell James, with nearly 100 illustrations. Their brave deeds from Lexington to Santiago, told in a captivating manner.

Uncle Tom's Cabin. By Harriet Beecher Stowe, with 50 illustrations. Arranged for young readers.

Sea Kings and Naval Heroes. By Hartwell James, with 50 illustrations.

Abbott's Historical Series.

PRICE, 50 CENTS EACH.

A well-known and popular series of biographical histories, by Jacob Abbott, containing the lives and deeds of founders of Empires, Heroes and Heroines of History, Kings, Queens and Conquerors.

Handsomely printed from large, clear type, on extra-fine super-calendered paper and embellished with half-tone frontispieces, numerous full-page and text illustrations and maps

... 1 **Romulus, the Founder of Rome.** With 49 illustrations.

... 2 **Cyrus the Great, the Founder of the Persian Empire.** With 40 illustrations.

... 3 **Darius the Great, King of the Medes and Persian.** With 34 illustrations.

... 4 **Xerxes the Great, King of Persia.** With 39 illustrations.

... 5 **Alexander the Great, King of Macedon.** With 51 illustrations.

... 6 **Pyrrhus, King of Epirus.** With 45 illustrations.

... 7 **Hannibal, the Carthaginian.** With 37 illustrations.

... 8 **Julius Cæsar, the Roman Conqueror.** With 44 illustrations.

... 9 **Alfred the Great, of England.** With 40 illustrations.

...10 **William the Conqueror, of England.** With 43 illustrations.

...11 **Hernando Cortez, the Conqueror of Mexico.** With 30 illustrations.

...12 **Mary, Queen of Scots.** With 45 illustrations.

...13 **Queen Elizabeth, of England.** With 49 illustrations.

...14 **King Charles the First, of England.** With 41 illustrations.

...15 **King Charles the Second, of England.** With 38 illustrations.

...16 **Maria Antoinette, Queen of France.** With 41 illustrations.

...17 **Madam Roland, A Heroine of the French Revolution.** With 42 illustrations.

...18 **Josephine, Empress of France.** With 40 illustrations.

ALTEMUS' DAINTY SERIES OF CHOICE GIFT BOOKS.

PRICE, 50 CENTS.

Bound in half-white Vellum, illuminated sides, unique design in gold, with numerous half-tone illustrations. Size, 6½ x 8 inches.

... 1 **The Silver Buckle.** By M. Nataline Crumpton. With 12 illustrations.

... 2 **Charles Dickens' Children Stories.** With 30 illustrations.

... 3 **The Children's Shakespeare.** With 30 illustrations.

... 4 **Young Robin Hood.** By G. Manville Fenn. With 30 illustrations.

... 5 **Honor Bright.** By Mary C. Rowsell. With 24 illustrations.

... 6 **The Voyage of the Mary Adair.** By Frances E. Crompton. With 19 illustrations.

... 7 **The Kingfisher's Egg.** By L. T. Meade. With 24 illustrations.

... 8 **Tattine.** By Ruth Ogden. With 24 illustrations.

... 9 **The Doings of a Dear Little Couple.** By Mary D. Brine. With 20 illustrations.

...10 **Our Soldier Boy.** By G. Manville Fenn. With 23 illustrations.

...11 **The Little Skipper.** By G. Manville Fenn. With 22 illustrations.

...12 **Little Gervaise and other Stories.** With 22 illustrations.

...13 **The Christmas Fairy.** By John Strange Winter. With 24 illustrations.

ALTEMUS' ILLUSTRATED DEVOTIONAL SERIES

An entirely new line of popular Religious Literature, carefully printed on fine paper, daintily and durably bound in handy volume size.

Full White Vellum, handsome new mosaic design in gold and colors, gold edges, boxed, 50 cents.

...32 **Message of Peace, The.** *Church.*

...33 **Morning Thoughts.** *Havergal.*

...34 **My King and His Service.** *Havergal.*

...35 **Natural Law in the Spiritual World.**
Drummond.

...37 **Pathway or Promise.**

...38 **Pathway of Safety.** *Oxenden.*

...39 **Peep of Day.**

...40 **Pilgrim's Progress, The.** *Bunyan.*

...41 **Precept Upon Precept.**

...42 **Prince of the House of David.** *Ingraham.*

...44 **Shepherd Psalm.** *Meyer.*

...45 **Steps Into the Blessed Life.** *Meyer.*

...46 **Stepping Heavenward.** *Prentiss.*

...47 **The Throne of Grace.**

...50 **With Christ.** *Murray.*

The Rise of the Dutch Republic (a History). By John Lothrop Motley. 55 full-page half-tone Engravings. Complete in two volumes—over 1,600 pages. Crown 8vo. Cloth, per set, $2.00. Half Morocco, gilt top, per set, $3 25.

Quo Vadis. A tale of the time of Nero, by Henryk Sienkiewicz. Complete and unabridged. Translated by Dr. S. A. Binion. Illustrated by M. De Lipman. Crown 8vo. Cloth, ornamental, 515 pages, $1.25.

With Fire and Sword. By the author of "Quo Vadis." A tale of the past. Illustrated. Crown 8vo. 825 pages, $1.00.

Pan Michael. By the author of "Quo Vadis." A historical tale. Illustrated. Crown 8vo. 530 pages, $1.00.

Julian, the Apostate. By S. Mereshkovski. Illustrated. Cloth 12mo. 450 pages, $1.00.

Manual of Mythology. For the use of Schools, Art Students, and General Readers, by Alexander S. Murray. With Notes, Revisions, and Additions by William H. Klapp. With 200 illustrations and an exhaustive Index. Large 12mo. Over 400 pages, $1.25.

The Age of Fable; or Beauties of Mythology. By Thomas Bulfinch, with Notes, Revisions, and Additions by William H. Klapp. With 200 illustrations and an exhaustive Index. Large 12mo. 450 pages, $1.25.

Stephen. A Soldier of the Cross. By Florence Morse Kingsley, author of "Titus, a Comrade of the Cross." Cloth, 12mo. 369 pages, $1.00.

The Cross Triumphant. By Florence Morse Kingsley, author of "Paul and Stephen." Cloth, 12mo. 364 pages, $1.00.

Paul. A Herald of the Cross. By Florence Morse Kingsley. Cloth, 12mo. 450 pages, $1.00.

The Pilgrim's Progress, as John Bunyan wrote it. A facsimile reproduction of the first edition, published in 1678. Antique cloth, 12mo. $1.25.

The Fairest of the Fair. By Hildegarde Hawthorne. Cloth, 16mo. $1.25.

Around the World in Eighty Minutes. Contains over 100 photographs of the most famous places and edifices, with descriptive text. Cloth, 50 cents.

Shakespeare's Complete Works. With 64 Boydell, and numerous other illustrations, four volumes, over 2,000 pages. Half Morocco, 12mo. Boxed, per set. $3.00.

The Care of Children. By Elizabeth R. Scovil. Cloth, 12mo. $1.00

Preparation for Motherhood. By Elizabeth R. Scovil. Cloth, 12mo. 320 pages, $1.00.

Baby's Requirements. By Elizabeth R. Scovil. Limp binding, leatherette. 25 cents.

Names for Children. By Elizabeth Robinson Scovil. Cloth, 12mo. 40 cents.

Trif and Trixy. By John Habberton, author of "Helen's Babies." Cloth, 12mo. 50 cents.

She Who Will Not When She May. By Eleanor G. Walton. Half-tone illustrations by C. P. M. Rumford. "An exquisite prose idyll." Cloth, gilt top, deckle edges. $1.00.

A Son of the Carolinas. By C. E. Satterthwaite. Cloth, 12mo. 280 pages, 50 cents.

What Women Should Know. By Mrs. E. B. Duffy. Cloth, 320 pages, 75 cents.

Dore Masterpieces.

The Dore Bible Gallery. Containing 100 full-page engravings by Gustave Dore.

Milton's Paradise Lost. With 50 full-page engravings by Gustave Dore.

Dante's Inferno. With 75 full-page engravings by Gustave Dore.

Dante's Purgatory and Paradise. With 60 full-page engravings by Gustave Dore.

Tennyson's Idylls of the King. With 37 full-page engravings by Gustave Dore.

The Rime of the Ancient Mariner. By Samuel Taylor Coleridge, with 46 full-page engravings by Gustave Dore. Cloth, ornamental, large quarto (9 x 12). Each $2.00.

Printed in Great Britain
by Amazon.co.uk, Ltd.,
Marston Gate.